W9-BRR-297

No Longer Silent

THE EMPOWERMENT OF WOMEN
IN THE GOSPELS

Susan Dehn Matthews

acta
PUBLICATIONS

NO LONGER SILENT
The Empowerment of Women in the Gospels
by Susan Dehn Matthews

Edited by Gregory F. Augustine Pierce
Cover design by Tom A. Wright
Cover artwork, "Wisdom," by James Fissel, used with permission
Text design and typesetting by Patricia Lynch

Unless otherwise noted, Scripture quotes are from the *New Revised Standard Version of the Bible*, copyright © 1989 by the Division of Christian Education of the National Council of the Churches of Christ in the USA. All rights reserved. Used with permission.

Copyright © 2011 by Susan Dehn Matthews

Published by ACTA Publications, 4848 N. Clark Street, Chicago, IL 60640, (800) 397-2282, www.actapublications.com

All rights reserved. No part of this publication may be reproduced or transmitted in any form or by any means, electronic or mechanical, including photocopying and recording, or by any information storage and retrieval system, including the Internet, without permission from the publisher. Permission is hereby given to use short excerpts with proper citation in reviews and marketing copy, church bulletins and handouts, and scholarly papers.

Library of Congress Catalog number: 2011909992
ISBN: 978-0-87946-470-7
Printed in the United States of America by McNaughton and Gunn
Year 20 19 18 17 16 15 14
Printing 15 14 13 12 11 10 9 8 7 6 5 4 3 2

CONTENTS

With gratitude for the women in my life
who shared Holy Wisdom with me
and taught me to listen deeply for her voice.

For my daughters, their children,
their children's children,
and all the generations to come,
so that they will hear the voices of these women
and thus be empowered to hear the Word
spoken within their own hearts.

PROLOGUE

This book came into existence in an intuitive fashion. I became aware of each woman's presence in the same way that you might see a person approaching in your peripheral vision. From this corner of my mind's eye—my heart's eye—these women drew me into a curious relationship with them. One by one, they introduced themselves to me and took me by the hand to lead me into their lives and the worlds they inhabited. They opened their hearts to me and allowed me to see through their eyes over the continuum of time and space. I stood with them before the man Jesus when he extended his human compassion, as well as his Wisdom and life energy, to them. The openness and friendship of these women have become invaluable to me and will, I hope, become similar gifts for you.

Each woman or group of women called to me and attracted my attention in a spontaneous and random order. Thus, there was no logical sequence in the writing of the book, nor should there be in the reading of it. My writing actually began at the end; your reading may begin somewhere in the middle. What is important is that you allow these ancient women to call to your heart and intrigue your mind with their voices and stories in the manner *they* choose to present themselves to you. Trust will be your companion and guide in meeting these women and listening to their voices. I am certain the moments when they encountered Jesus and were empowered to know their own portion of the Divine life within, the moments when the women understood their power and place in Creation, and the moments when they discovered their own interior Wisdom will resonate within you precisely when you need them the most.

This book should be read without mindfulness of chronological time. Rather, immerse yourself in *kairos,* the Divine suspension of the constraints of time as we know it. Imagine, visualize, listen, and reflect. Spend time with the questions presented at the end of each chapter for personal reflection and—if you are fortunate—discussion with others, and be aware of other questions and thoughts that arise within you. Be especially present to the moments when *you* are face to face with Jesus and feel the stirrings of Divine energy. Give yourself permission to be led on a journey within and beyond what you thought possible. Savor the opportunity to complete the journeys of these women with your own.

My hope and prayer is that you will be blessed by these women, and by the One who respected and blessed their existence and empowered them to live creatively and fully in the world.

Susan Dehn Matthews
Plainfield, Illinois

INTRODUCTION

There are the familiar, remembered stories from the gospels—the stories we hear over and over as the readings of the liturgical cycles revolve and recur. While few in number, the stories that concern women are not unfamiliar. We know the mother of Jesus, Mary Magdalene, and the woman at the well—or at least we think we do. Their stories, however, have been distilled to well-worn themes and only select details about them have been emphasized as worthy of our attention or emulation.

Yet many moments in their stories go unnoticed and forgotten, begging the question of why this happened. Close examination of what is written—and unwritten—overwhelmingly reveals a deliberate elimination or exclusion of the portions of their stories that concern each woman's empowerment. To reveal these women as they became awakened to the power of the Divine within themselves, as they were radically changed and as they moved forward into the world as agents of their own change, would be like playing with fire. It would undermine the presumed dependence of the women in the gospels and dispel the myth of their inferior human and spiritual status. If people hear more complete accounts of these women's lives, they might be at risk of similar transformation and change—an unacceptable possibility from the patriarchal point of view.

There is more, however. There are women who have been ignored altogether in the Scriptures. They are the unnamed and invisible. In some cases, these women have been and still are assumed to be men in the context of the overwhelmingly masculine perspective and imagery of the Scriptures. These are the women whose stories have not been told because they were not recognized as worthy of telling in anything more than a cursory fashion. Our presumptions need to be put aside.

The moments when women discovered within themselves the Divine energy that forever altered the course of their lives and empowered them to live from this newly realized center of their being—these moments of change are the stories worthy of being retold in a new framework or, perhaps, recovered for the first time. By changing the vantage point of our perspective from masculine to feminine, the stories of these women unfold before us as a new articulation of Jesus' own vision: *The kingdom of God is within you* (Luke 17:21). Each woman whose story is recounted here is remarkable precisely because, through the power of an encounter with Jesus, she discovered within herself the Divine energy that allowed her to offer her unique gift to the world. Recognized and validated by Jesus, each woman was empowered with the freedom, wholeness and self-awareness needed to birth her unique contribution into the world, for the good of all Creation, through the struggles and limitations of her life.

The portraits offered here attempt to give voice to the minds and hearts of these women of the gospels. While their exact, personal circumstances have been lost to us, either minimized or omitted from the text entirely, it is possible to reconstruct the flavor and tone of their time based on sound biblical scholarship. It is another matter, however, to hear the voices of their minds and hearts. Very little is preserved for us to listen to, and we have been conditioned to hear these precious few words as devoid of human emotion. Where no words exist, we have been lulled into envisioning the women as detached, passive, silent observers of their own lives. Much about these gospel women has been ignored, forgotten, and silenced.

To listen for their voices with fresh ears requires a certain audacity. It requires listening to your own heart and defying convention. Openness to new possibilities must be conceived, while raw emotions must be recognized and inserted into their narratives. A renewed understanding of Jesus should include his radical empowerment of women and his respect for their gifts as integral to the unfolding of Creation. The stories that flow from the minds and hearts of these women are worthy of our personal reflection precisely because they will assist us in discerning how this same Divine energy flows within *us*—women and men alike. The witness of these women offers us the infinite possibility that, through the ordinary circumstances of our lives, we too can be empowered and transformed by the Divine spark that exists within us. By playing with fire, we can choose the abundance of life intended for all of humanity from the beginning of Creation.

Their voices still resonate. *Let anyone with ears to hear listen!* (Luke 8:8)

Creation Within

ELIZABETH

When Elizabeth heard Mary's greeting,
the child leaped in her womb.
And Elizabeth was filled with the Holy Spirit
and exclaimed with a loud cry,
"Blessed are you among women,
and blessed is the fruit of your womb.
And why has this happened to me,
that the mother of my Lord comes to me?
For as soon as I heard the sound of your greeting,
the child in my womb leaped for joy.
And blessed is she who believed
that there would be a fulfillment
of what was spoken to her by the Lord."

Luke 1:41-45

The firmament overhead always seemed to mock her in the silence of the night. She found it difficult to look at the myriad lights of heaven, splashed across the bowl of the sky. To do so only brought the Lord's words to her mind and heart: *Look toward heaven and count the stars, if you are able to count them. So shall your descendents be.* Just like her foremother, Sarah, she laughed derisively at the improbability of this promise. *Why, Lord? Perhaps this was possible in my youth, but no longer. I am an old woman, barren with the years. My body tired of holding hope long ago; even the moon has abandoned her grasp on me. Yet, you remind me each evening of my shame and emptiness. Why, Lord?*

This was a prayer born of exhaustion and disappointment. She had only desired to give her husband what every woman wanted: a son, a child. *Of all the stars above my head, is there not one that bears the name of my child? Am I to forever mourn the child for whom there is no promised star?* Her questions seemed to go unheeded, unanswered, as if the Lord hid behind the sky itself. Yet she knew love with her husband, not rejection. Together they lived according to the commandments and honored the priestly traditions of their ancestors. They carved out a portion of the world for themselves and grew old in its comforting familiarity. It was not what they had longed for, but it was enough.

Her husband's service in the Temple interrupted the comfort of his presence more often than she liked. In the early years, she traveled with him; however, as the years wore on she remained at home, as the journey was tiresome for her. Yet her encouragement of and pride in her husband's priestly duties never faltered. She listened eagerly with open heart and ears to his every telling of what he saw, heard, smelled and felt in the Temple. Even after all these years, she loved the sound of his voice.

Months ago, however, even his voice was taken from her. This time, there were no stories when he returned from the Temple, only gestures she could not interpret. *Lord, for what purpose have you emptied my life? There is so little left for an old woman like me!* Perhaps it was her deep sadness that prompted her husband to take her into his bed in the quiet of the night. Yes, there was little left, but there were still some pleasures to enjoy as husband and wife. And so, in the solace and comfort of their love, they discovered there was still some measure of joy to be found under the silent presence of the stars.

From that night forward, subtle reminders of her advancing age began to make themselves known. Fatigue and discomfort announced her increasing limitations; her belly felt heavy and her breasts hung low. *If I were a young woman, these would be signs that I am with child. How strange that in my wisdom years, my body would remind me so cruelly of my disgrace.* Gradually, seclusion enveloped her within her own home and there were hours upon hours in which to reflect on the changes she experienced.

Over time, her body became more sensitive to the subtleties of this circumscribed world. The fragrances of bread and wine, of fruits and flowers, became more intense and held nuances she never discerned before. The winds weaving through the hills smelled of far-off salty seas and filled her with their presence. Even the night stars seemed to give up their mockery and shine more brightly for her—perhaps even within her. Disappointment gave way gradually to an awareness of being part of something much larger and more mysterious. The rhythm and heartbeat of Creation pulsated within her. And then, one day, she laughed. *Could it be? Am I to bear a child? May I be favored by the Lord!*

Still uncertain that she could dare to hope, the visit of her young kinswoman was a welcome diversion. Word had come only days before, and the hasty preparations had exacted a price from the old woman. Tired and worn, she waited under the shade of the gnarled tree in the courtyard, from where she would see the approach of her kinswoman.

As the morning's coolness gave way to the rising sun, she heard the young woman's voice raised in greeting and, in that instant, the whole of Creation moved within her. In the space of a breath, she became aware of a holy presence, concentrated within her kinswoman's body, moving powerfully through everything that surrounded her. In that instant, she realized the whole of Creation was responding in recognition. The winds reverently abated. Light sparkled on the precious liquid in the water jars. Her heart beat faster. The child within her moved. *Why has this happened to me, that the mother of my Lord comes to me?*

This was her moment of profound fulfillment and grace. She was face-to-face with Life and was being drawn into the delicate balance of its relationship with all of Creation. Meeting the unseen child awakened within her the very energy that enlivened all of Creation and connected her to its Source. *The star I longed for was never in the sky! The star I have desired was held within my self, full of promise and life, waiting to be called forth into relationship with my Lord. In this there is no disgrace!*

FOR REFLECTION

What do I perceive as impossible in my life? What does my willingness to lose hope reveal to me?

What place do disappointment and anger have in my life? In what ways have I grown or been stunted through my experience of these emotions?

Am I ever tempted to succumb to the excuse of being unable to be full of life? What circumstances cause me to feel barren and empty?

When have I looked outside myself for identity and fulfillment? What were the circumstances that prompted me to do this?

How have I been drawn into life-giving relationship with God and the whole of Creation? What portion of myself am I willing to invest in this relationship?

The Reflective Woman

MARY OF NAZARETH

They made known
what had been told them
about this child;
and all who heard it were amazed
at what the shepherds told them.

But Mary treasured all these words
and pondered them in her heart.

Luke 2:17-19

The events of the past several months surprised and confused her. She needed time away in hopes of allowing the advent of this new reality to fully settle into comfortable familiarity. And so she traveled into the hill country to assist with her cousin's pregnancy, as much as to learn from it—for her youth was a blessing but her inexperience a danger. On the way, she inwardly marveled at the subtle changes already wrought in her body: the sense of heaviness in her breasts and the small, almost imperceptible but pleasant, sensations of bubbles bursting within her belly. She laughed quietly at these first stirrings of the child within.

While there were many tasks to keep her busy in her cousin's home, there were quiet moments as well. She walked in the gardens and looked up into the starlit night sky, aware of the seemingly infinite varieties of Creation. She spoke to her unborn child and placed a tender hand against her increasingly taut skin in reassurance of her love and protection, envisioning that someday she would nourish this child and steady his first steps by holding his small hands.

Day followed day, moon succeeded moon, and with them came a burgeoning sense of well-being and contentment in her mind and heart. Upon returning home, whatever doubt she had harbored about her betrothed's response to her condition was swept away; in some ways she felt as though she had only dreamed of fear and rejection. As her body swelled, so too did her imagination; she pictured in great detail the life growing within her. Eyes, ears, nose, mouth, fingers, toes…*the Lord who made you, who formed you in the womb*…the words of the prophet Isaiah resounded often in her heart. *How delicate the hand of the Creator to fashion the tiny, intricate parts of my infant son! How well he is already known and cherished by our God, named even before placed in my womb, according to God's word.* His name filled her with hope as she contemplated the future and drew her hand around her undulating belly in spiraling circles of blessing. *Jesus…Jesus…Jesus….*

The words of the announcement that she was to bear a son commanded little of her youthful attention at first, as the unfolding of new life took hold within her womb. Unable to comprehend the magnitude of birthing the Son of the Most High, the One who would regain the throne of their ancestor David, her awareness had naturally been drawn inward by the more urgent demands of the growing child. Yet the message would surface during the times just before sleep, as she succumbed to the increasing fatigue of her pregnancy, and float back to her conscious mind as she awakened. As the time of her confinement drew near, she pondered what these words would demand of her and assessed the answering virtues and strengths she possessed, wondering if they would be sufficient for the task. However, above all else, she listened. She listened with the full measure of her energy and spirit for the Divine voice that would guide her in this undertaking.

What she did not anticipate was an arduous journey to the place where she would give birth to her son. Listening had not required the sheer physical strength she needed now to coax her body to endure the reverberations that ran up her spine with every step and caused the child within to writhe and push against the constraint of her body. In listening to her body and to her unborn son, however, she became acutely aware of the imminence of her son's appearance in the world. She desired nothing more than warmth and shelter in which to deliver this child of God into the safekeeping of her arms.

Birth was rarely a private affair; kinswomen and midwives, women of wisdom and experience, guided a new mother in the art of birthing and welcomed the newborn with practiced hands. *Why am I alone in this labor, Holy Wisdom? Where are those who would serve you in bringing forth your son? Is there no one to attend his birth?*

Her journey culminated in the City of David, at the threshold of an inn where she and her husband hoped to find respite from the road. The innkeeper was herself a brusque and hardened woman, but a woman nonetheless. One look told her everything she needed to know: birth was imminent and, judging from the youth of this mother, there was a need for privacy. The inn, with its crush of humanity, would not provide the hospitality required to comfort a fearful woman and provide sanctuary for a child so new to the world. With the gentleness of a midwife, the innkeeper created a comfortable space with clean straw and water in the stable of her establishment—hovering over the birth, making small reassuring noises, and receiving the young woman's gift of a first-born son in arms that had held many newborn creatures before.

Exhausted and emptied, the young mother considered the innkeeper's deportment. *Look at this woman's tenderness, her recognition of how sacred life is. Her gentleness lies hidden in a rough exterior, much like a precious stone. See how she welcomes the unexpected with such openness! I am so grateful for her presence and faithful attention. She has assisted me in bringing forth my son safely, and has helped to birth me as a mother. God, you are gracious!* She settled into quiet reflection, lulled by the breathing of child, husband and animals, until sleep stole over her.

New sounds of whispers and feet shuffling in the straw awakened her some time later. Through the liminal haze of sleep, she saw women and children lingering at the door to the stable, accompanied by the fresh fragrance of grass and open fields. *Shepherds, by the look of them; why are they here?* She looked to her husband, but finding no answer in his face, she turned once more toward the small assembly before her. They gazed in awe at the child slumbering peacefully nearby. Then, like the beginning of a gentle spring rain, words began to drop from their mouths, clear and reverent, opening her heart just as rain opens the soil. *Do not be afraid…good news…great joy for all the people…Savior…Messiah…Lord…a sign…lying in a manger.* Turning to her son, she entered the awed wonder of those present to contemplate the blessings bestowed in the tiny form of the infant before her. The words of the Creation story permeated her consciousness and struck a new chord within her heart: *This at last is bone of my bones and flesh of my flesh…. This one shall be called man, for out of woman this one was taken.*

Raising her eyes, she smiled at those drawn into the circle of her child's presence — the poor, the simple, the innocent. She pondered the great power of her small son to touch their hearts. These were human beings open to imagination and possibility, capable of recognizing the genuine face of love and receptive enough to allow this infant's nascent power to grow in the fertile soil of their lives. She understood the effect of her son's energy on these women and children because she had come to know it herself and participated as it unfolded in the world. Such was the Wisdom shared with her that night, to be treasured and held precious in all the days to come.

FOR REFLECTION

How do I sense the interconnectedness of my body, mind and spirit? In which sphere do I tend to dwell; which sphere requires greater integration from me in order to achieve balance?

What do I need to change in my life in order to take the time to be attentive and listen carefully to all the voices that speak to me? What level of risk am I willing to take in order to invest myself in the process of change?

As I assess the virtues and strengths I possess, do I wonder if they will be sufficient for the arduous journey of my life? What insights or wisdom about myself become apparent as I consider the person I am now and the person I hope to become?

Am I willing to conceive of and labor toward bringing about the world as it could be? Have I emptied myself enough to allow alternative visions to energize me?

In the emergent pattern of the universe, do I see myself giving birth to the Christ and completing a portion of the cyclical pattern that will continue long after I am gone? What does having a Christic-consciousness mean in my daily life?

Grace and Vision

ANNA

There was also a prophet, Anna the daughter of Phanuel, of the tribe of Asher. She was of a great age, having lived with her husband seven years after her marriage, then as a widow to the age of eighty-four. She never left the temple but worshiped there with fasting and prayer night and day. At that moment she came, and began to praise God and to speak about the child to all who were looking for the redemption of Jerusalem.

Luke 2:36-38

Sitting in the precincts of the Temple each day, she had many hours for reflection on the memories of a full life, which once included a husband and family. Her eyes followed the shadows cast by the columns of the Temple porticoes as they moved slowly across the paving stones in front of her. In much the same way, her constant prayer devoted attentiveness to the movement of the Divine within her old and wise heart. Her recollection of the past and the Wisdom wrought through experience evoked her prophetic awareness. She allowed her mind to wander back and forth over the course of her life. Remaining present to the insights and revelations gleaned from her own length of days, as well as to the stories and traditions handed down from her ancestors, demanded the whole of her existence now. *I am an old woman. My body aches during prayer and my hunger distracts me. How do I remain vigilant and present to the ways in which the Divine appears before me when my energy drains away so quickly and I am susceptible not only to the chill of the evening, but to the heat of the noonday sun as well?*

Yet the deeper energies of grace and vision sustained her, much as it had for those who preceded her. *My ancestors were the people of Asher, descendents of Jacob and Zilpah, the servant of Leah. Asher's name gave honor to the god of his mother, the god to whom the Temple of the Universe was dedicated. Among Jacob's many children, the people of Asher were the ones set apart by their honor not only for the God of Jacob, but for that of Zilpah. Over many generations, the tribe of Asher set themselves apart by clinging both to the territory along the seacoast and to the traditions of the goddess. My foremothers and fathers resisted the call of Deborah and Barak to move against the Canaanite people — who were as much their own flesh and blood as was Israel. The name of my father — Phanuel — bears the imprint of the struggle between Jacob and the Divine One, in which Jacob met God face-to-face. My own experience is exactly that — a struggle to search for and discover the face of the Divine.*

Soon, she would join those who preceded her. She had known the blessing of a husband for seven years, and lived on for twelve times that to reach the wisdom of her eighty-four years. The significance of her great age was not lost on her. *The numbers seven and twelve reveal a time of completion for me and for my people — the time of redemption for Jerusalem, the restoration of an age of peace. Deep in my old bones, I feel that a moment of great revelation is near.*

She chose to live, worship, and give prophetic witness within the Temple in Jerusalem, because it embodied the complex revelation of the Divine that was her heritage. Long ago, the central rock within the Temple Mount was dedicated to the Canaanite goddess Asherah, as she was known to the people of Israel, just as now it was the dwelling place of Israel's Yahweh. *Even Solomon, in honor of his wife's household, erected a shrine to the goddess in this place. Where else would I find myself at home when I am so far from my homeland? It will be in a place such as this that the God of the Universe will be revealed to me.*

A long life had prepared her to wait upon God with patience. Each day, she watched as the heart of the world throbbed before her. Poverty was assuaged by alms. Intercessions were offered for healing. Students sought knowledge. Parents presented their first-born sons to the Lord. The rhythm of the days and nights varied only with the festivals and seasons, even while faces changed with every hour. It was in the very usual cadence of such a day that two parents, ordinary in their demeanor, brought their tiny son to the Temple for presentation and dedication — an event that caused her to feel the collective heartbeat of the world quicken around her.

She was not alone in this awareness. Another figure, a man — Simeon — who was himself open to the Spirit, reached for the child and praised God that he had lived to see the light of revelation. Now the prophetess moved closer to the child as the parents looked on, amazed at the power of attraction their child possessed for her. The ancient flesh and bone of her body, full of memory and presence, gravitated to this newborn and the grace of Divine Life filled her spirit. *This is the longed-for Messiah. This is the moment of peace and Divine revelation I have so eagerly anticipated!*

Trusting the urging of the Spirit, she began to share the truth of what was unfolding in the course of this ordinary day with anyone who would listen. She proclaimed the God of the Universe to all who could hear her voice.

The ancient Wisdom she had held close through all of her days and nights was brought to fulfillment. There were indeed many ways in which the One God revealed Self. And, just as the patriarch Jacob did so long ago, she, too, met God face-to-face, and lived.

FOR REFLECTION

When am I most aware of God's presence in my life? In the world? In the universe?

Where is God present to me in the ordinary rhythms of my daily life? In what ways is my search for God a struggle?

Do I value what the various people of the world tell me about the face of God? In what ways has my own image of God evolved and grown because of these revelations?

Am I willing to acknowledge that my understanding of God is fragmentary and incomplete? Do I experience resonance or resistance to the idea that I must listen to the voices of all people as they share their pieces of the truth about the One God of the Universe with me?

Where have I met God face-to-face? Am I able to proclaim my God?

Outspoken Boldness

MARY IN THE TEMPLE

After three days they found him in the temple, sitting among the teachers, listening to them and asking them questions. And all who heard him were amazed at his understanding and his answers. When his parents saw him they were astonished; and his mother said to him, "Child, why have you treated us like this? Look, your father and I have been searching for you in great anxiety." He said to them, "Why were you searching for me? Did you not know that I must be in my Father's house?" But they did not understand what he said to them. Then he went down with them and came to Nazareth, and was obedient to them. His mother treasured all these things in her heart. And Jesus increased in wisdom and in years, and in divine and human favor.

Luke 2:46-52

Train children in the right way, and when old, they will not stray. The words were ancient, but the wisdom had served her well as a young mother. Her child had an inclination toward willfulness, the inevitable result of an active and creative mind, as well as a strong and independent spirit. Most times, a look or a few well-chosen words sufficed for discipline, often stirring wonder and amazement among the other mothers of Nazareth, who resorted to heavier hands in dealing with their own headstrong offspring. What made her subdued admonishment possible was the relationship shared between mother and son—a love grounded in deep mutual respect. For any mother to love a daughter or son was expected; yet, not all were able to recognize the gift of Divine energy within their children and grant them their inherent dignity, as she did her son. By doing so, she imparted Wisdom far more ancient than that contained in the venerable Book of Proverbs.

By acknowledging the sacredness of his life, she taught her son to appreciate the value of life in all of its manifestations and guises. She attended to the hungry and the voiceless, while at the same time she possessed a tremendous capacity to marvel at the intricacy of a tender leaf unfolding and to revel in the antics of a newborn, bleating lamb. She poured her life out as a gift to everything and everyone she encountered, and in turn taught her son to do the same. She spent time in reflective quiet, alone with her God, and thus taught her child to pray in places other than the synagogue, in the places where her mother and foremothers sought the Divine—within the solitude of a garden, under the whispering leaves in a grove of trees, on a windblown hilltop, and upon the waters of the lake. She helped her son feel the immanent presence of Yahweh's Hokmah—the manifold and unique Wisdom of God's spirit—by guiding his eyes and heart to see and rejoice in the surprising, playful, creative spirit of God.

Each year, as the fig trees yielded their first fruits of the year and lambs appeared in the fields, she made preparations for her family to travel to Jerusalem for the Passover festival. Provisions for the journey were assembled among the members of their extended family and, when all was in readiness, they all made their way to Jerusalem. These were relaxed and joyous times, with opportunity for conversation or quiet thoughts among the adults while the children romped and roamed within sight of the larger group. Occasionally, she caught sight of her son and smiled inwardly at his ambivalence—one minute engaged in the latest antics of the children, the next tagging just behind and listening solemnly to the conversations of the men, nodding in agreement with some proffered opinion. *Look at him! He stands on the cusp of adulthood and I am so proud of the man he is becoming; but, oh, how I wish I could hold him just as he is for a while longer. Why does a mother need to surrender her child over and over, first from her body and then again and again to independence? Have I done enough to prepare him for his work in the world?*

The same thoughts and questions returned to her over the course of the journey and the time her family spent in Jerusalem. She saw Jesus' excitement and intrigue as he engaged with the larger world—all the more evident this year than ever before. *He is filled with an energetic spirit that seeks to reveal itself to the world. How can I possibly hold on to him much longer? And yet, I want to protect him from the dangers every man and woman must face. We live between two worlds, in tension between the law of Yahweh and the law of Rome. Do I simply resign myself to his fate—whatever that will be? Don't I have some influence in these matters?* Influence was exactly what she desired.

The days of the Passover complete, the entire extended family began the long road back to Nazareth, eager to return to the familiarity of home. As the hours and miles passed in succession, however, an anxiety settled over her when there was no sign of Jesus. Her kinswomen assured her that he must be with others in the group: Where else could he be? *True, he was with us as we gathered to start our homeward travel. Yet, I have not seen him with either the children or the men. He has not appeared for meals, nor has he slept at our fire. Does no one know of his where-abouts?* She questioned her husband, who in turn sought their son among their kinsmen. She went among the women and the older children, but to no avail. *Gracious and loving God, where is he? Is he injured? Lost? Has he been abducted by robbers or wild animals? I trust him to your hand, God. Do not disappoint me! I beg you to hold him fast in your sure grasp!*

Anxiety turned to panic as she gathered her things and shook off the reassuring hand of her husband. She started to walk back the way they had come, ignoring the imploring requests of others to wait and look further for her son within the camps of their extended family. *I will not be dissuaded. He must be found! Come if you want to or stay behind, but I will go! I will find my son!* She strode back along the road determinedly, leaving her husband no option but to trail behind.

Arriving once more in Jerusalem, they combed the lanes and markets near the place where they had stayed. *Nothing! My God, where can he be? I still feel hope within my breast; there is no sense of loss and desolation. I am sure he lives, but where, where O God, is he? How dare he take advantage of our trust? How could he disregard his mother's heart? He has not learned well enough the lesson of respect for his parents! A man does not disregard the welfare of his family!*

There was no place they had not searched — save for the Temple. More than seven days had passed since she had last set eyes on Jesus, which caused her to move with even more desperation and haste as she turned toward the Temple Mount. Her husband begged her to be more reserved in her movements, to observe the propriety expected within the Temple precincts. With frantic eyes she searched her husband's face for understanding, even as they approached the *mikvah* where they would ritually wash before ascending the staircase to the outer courtyard of the Temple above.

No sooner was this accomplished than she moved quickly up the wide staircase with the assumption that her husband would follow. She saw no faces on the people she passed, nor did she notice the great number of stairs. Her attention lay in what was beyond. *Where can he have gone? If he is here, will he linger in the porticoes or advance to the inner courtyards? Would he look for me in the Court of the Women and linger there in hopes of my return? Would he dare to go farther into the Temple than is allowed?*

Advancing farther and farther into the Temple area, she saw him at last—a crowd of onlookers gathered around him. He was speaking, and she noticed the rapt attention of the teachers as they listened to him, nodding in amazement at and acknowledgement of the Wisdom he possessed. For an instant, her emotions abated and she stood still, as if rooted to the pavement and unable to move. Then, her heart swelled with pride in her child. He was almost a man: *Almost, but not yet.* She shook herself, as if coming awake, and moved forward through the crowd intent on reaching her son.

Only when she stopped directly in front of him did she realize that she had advanced beyond the Courtyard of the Women, so that she now stood among the rabbis and other men who were engaged with her son in learned exchange. *O God, give me strength! I tremble in front of all with relief and pride, with anger and fatigue—they will think me a weak woman who does not know her place.* Summoning her maternal courage, she spoke directly to her son: *Child, why have you treated us like this? Look, your father and I have been searching for you in great anxiety.* She heard those gathered murmur and gasp at the insult of a woman who would speak so peremptorily and publicly in front of her own husband. The sounds quelled as her son responded: *Why were you searching for me? Did you not know that I must be in my Father's house?* As one, those assembled turned to look at her, as much to put her in her place as to hope for a response. The true meaning of Jesus' words baffled her, but not the intention behind them. She knew the child who so desperately wanted to be a man, who desired purpose and recognition. And she could imagine the man he was becoming.

She gestured for her son to follow and together, with her husband, they moved to leave the Temple and return home. There was so much yet to teach her son, so much Wisdom to be shared…some of which she had just become aware of within herself.

FOR REFLECTION

What are the greatest revelations of Wisdom I have received in my life? Is my heart open to new and surprising sources of Wisdom?

In what ways am I aware of my own inner child? How do I seek to satisfy my need to learn, to test, to be surprised and to marvel at Creation?

What do I seek to control in my life? Do I seek control because I doubt the effectiveness of my own strengths and gifts?

What causes me anxiety and worry? Is it possible for me to approach these circumstances in a more life-affirming manner?

Is boldness one of my gifts? How far do I dare to go in response to my own true nature?

Feast of Recognition

MARY AT THE WEDDING OF CANA

On the third day there was a wedding in Cana of Galilee, and the mother of Jesus was there. Jesus and his disciples had also been invited to the wedding. When the wine gave out, the mother of Jesus said to him, "They have no wine." And Jesus said to her, "Woman, what concern is that to you and to me? My hour has not yet come." His mother said to the servants, "Do whatever he tells you."

Jesus did this, the first of his signs, in Cana of Galilee, and revealed his glory.

John 2:1-5, 11

Mothers are gifted with the awareness of a child's being long before the child is capable of self-awareness. She was aware since this child's conception that she carried a rare and precious treasure within her body. Tears welcomed the child's presence within her—tears of joy, of fear, of relief, of foreboding. She held the secret of her child for some time, cherishing their private bond, reluctant to acknowledge its existence to others. Even in those early days, when they shared the hospitality of her body, she came to know her child intimately in a way that no one else ever would.

Through the years, as her child grew in strength and filled with Wisdom, she recognized the favor of God upon him. She listened carefully to the words of all who encountered the child, and she alone understood with her mother's heart how he would be called to a greatness that few could ever truly grasp. She watched his play, saw his efforts in reading the Scriptures, endured his grumbling about chores, and relished his generous, smiling spirit when it sprang forth spontaneously. It was his inward struggle, however, to become who God intended him to be that hinted to her of his calling. *Only a person called to great work grapples as he does to find harmony and peace of spirit within.* She understood that what seemed like daydreaming to others was in truth his prayer. His wandering among the hills and groves seemed an evasion of responsibility, but she knew his heart was troubled with the discernment of knowing his true identity and purpose in life. She ached with her own inability to ease his heart. Once she could comfort his distress with a word or embrace—but no longer, now that he had reached maturity. She knew him. She knew that he was a child of the living God. But she did not yet recognize how the truth of who he was would be expressed.

If mothers have knowledge and wisdom, they also possess their suspicions and insights. Many times she witnessed his compassion for children and small creatures, or his simple pleasure at running an open hand over the barley heads that waved in the breeze. It was obvious to her that, when he looked to the heavens, he saw beyond the winnowing fan of the stars. She felt his connection to Creation and the Creator, almost as if her son was still one with her physically. She heard his impatience with those who revered the Law over the welfare of the people. And she smiled. Hers was a pleasure and pride that reveled in the goodness of her son, the child of her body.

His joys were hers, like they are for any mother. When he laughed or danced or threw himself into celebrations wholeheartedly, his energy passed from person to person as he joined in their merriment. In anticipation of this sharing, she looked forward to the evening's wedding feast in Cana, where she would see her son after his journey beyond the Jordan and through the Galilee. *Has he changed since I saw him last? I have heard that many follow him now from place to place. What is it that attracts them to his side?*

At last, from her place among the women, she saw him arrive. In the midst of the music and dancing, his eyes searched the guests for her face and lit with warmth and love when he found hers. She returned his smile with one that told of the depth of her love for him. Family and friends, full of conviviality, welcomed him with an invitation to recline at table along with those who accompanied him. Though impatient, she reassured herself: *There is time enough. We will talk later, in private, when the days of these festivities have been completed and all return to their homes.*

Food and drink were abundant, and the wedding guests did not shy away from partaking of the host's generosity. Eventually, as the hours passed, the wine gave out. This caused grumbling among the company and pressured the hospitality of the host, who sent out inquiries to obtain any supply that might satisfy. Feeling great empathy for the potential embarrassment of the host, she wondered if her son might move to remedy the situation. She found him, however, engaged in animated conversation and oblivious to the predicament. As she looked at him, memories of his childhood flooded her mind. She recalled moments that were surprising and full of mystery—never fully explained to her by her son. Pressed for answers, he had simply grinned or shrugged his shoulders, as if to dismiss the possibility that there was anything unusual about whatever turn of events had just occurred. The same awe and wonder she had felt in those times resurfaced now. Her suspicions solidified into recognition of the truth of his identity. *Why does he ignore those who are in need at this time of joy and festivity? Rise from your place, my son! Act now; this is the appointed hour!*

She was unable to attract his attention. *He must see my gestures, yet he ignores me like a little one who does not want to be called in from play! If I do not act with urgency now, the moment will be lost.* Crossing the banquet space, she approached her son from the side. Standing near to him, she whispered: *They have no wine.* In a tone of like confidence, he replied without looking at her: *Woman, what concern is that to you and to me? My hour has not yet come.* Realizing both his reluctance and his readiness as only a mother could, her thoughts drifted back to the moment of his birth. *My son, once long ago you chose your time to enter the world. It is now the moment for me to choose to birth you once again, for I know of your strength and your readiness, even if I do not know my own.* Turning to the servants, she spoke aloud: *Do whatever he tells you.*

He looked at her, glancing from her face to the water jars at hand. There was a quiet pause, similar to the suspension of time between expelling a child from one's body and the instant when its first cry is uttered. In that space, there exists both hope and fear—and she held her breath as she waited. *How will his life unfold because of what I have just done?* Tears of trepidation welled in her eyes. Then, she heard the words of his response: *Fill the jars with water!* Suddenly, in the midst of this joyous occasion, all of the prophetic words that she treasured in her heart broke open with unsuspected power. *God, you have opened my eyes and I now recognize who he truly is. I have birthed the Anointed One into the world. I give you glory, my God, and celebrate that you have invited me once again to reply to you with a resounding Yes.* Entering into this consciousness, her tears were transformed into drops of liquid joy.

FOR REFLECTION

How capable am I of recognizing the revelations of God placed before my eyes? What doubts do I have about the authenticity of these disclosures?

Based upon my life experience thus far, what do I suspect is my role in birthing the Divine into the world? Why do I trust or dismiss my insights?

What is my capacity for participating in the labor of birthing Christic-consciousness into the world? What do I fear are my inadequacies?

What depth of intimacy exists in my relationship with Jesus the Christ? How am I revealed to myself through this relationship?

Am I capable of living the Truth, as it is revealed to me in the most unlikely places and circumstances of life? Where or when might this be the most difficult for me to live authentically?

Thirst Quenched

THE SAMARITAN WOMAN

It was about noon. A Samaritan woman came to draw water, and Jesus said to her, "Give me a drink…." The Samaritan woman said to him, "How is it that you, a Jew, ask a drink of me, a woman of Samaria?"

Jesus answered her, "If you knew the gift of God, and who it is that is saying to you, 'Give me a drink,' you would have asked him, and he would have given you living water."

The woman said to him, "I know that Messiah is coming" (who is called Christ). "When he comes, he will proclaim all things to us." Jesus said to her, "I am he, the one who is speaking to you." Just then his disciples came. They were astonished that he was speaking with a woman.

Then the woman left her water jar and went back to the city. She said to the people, "Come and see a man who told me everything I have ever done!"

John 4: 6-7, 9-10, 25-29

She went to draw water at mid-day when she would not be confronted by the other women who filled their jars as the light of morning dawned. Her life was difficult; she had gone from one relationship to another searching for something—what, she didn't know. Over the years, with each relationship that came and went, she moved herself farther and farther from the company of others—ashamed and unsure of their suspicions and judgments, fearful of their sharp tongues.

On this day, as she looked up from her task, a stranger appeared, asking her simply for a drink of water. Defying convention, she looked into the eyes of this man she did not know and sensed something she had never encountered before. Unable to name her feelings, yet with her awareness piqued, she responded defensively to his request: *Why are you asking me, a woman, a foreigner, for a drink? Where is your own bucket and cup? Yet if I do not draw the water and serve you, your thirst will continue.* His look was gentle. He pursued the line of questioning further: *Who are you? Who is your husband? What do you need?*

He then began to tell her about her life—the details, the nuances. Her soul was moved, and she reeled in confusion. *How does this stranger know me, know the truth of my fragmented and imperfect life?* There was power in the words he spoke; his was a knowing and piercing confrontation. Still afraid, yet intrigued, the words escaped her mouth before she could stifle them and, with a boldness born from the fatigue of oppression, she challenged him and threw away the shackles of propriety: *Where should one worship—in the place of our ancestors or in Jerusalem?* As she pursued this bold dialogue, unspoken questions arose within her, vying for her annoyed attention. *What is it about this man that provokes me to such courage—or utter foolishness? Why am I so audacious in my manner? Who am I, indeed: a woman of shame and trepidation or a woman of strength and surety? Could this be the One who was promised, the One who would redeem the people from all of their divisions and slaveries? Why does he choose to enter a dialogue with me, a woman whose very presence is said to defile?* The questions within choked her as if they were sands driven before a windstorm, and created a thirst for answers that could not be assuaged by ordinary water.

Suddenly, in the desperation of that moment, the Wisdom submerged in the depths of her heart broke forth. It surged and bubbled to the surface of her consciousness. *I feel it; this must be the Spirit of Truth he speaks of and the Living Water he offers! My questions and challenges have led me to the inner depths of truth for which I have been searching! I have something of value to offer the world.*

They were still locked in the embrace of dialogue when their conversation was interrupted with the return of the disciples, who surrounded them in amazement and wonder, incredulous at what they witnessed with their own eyes and heard with their own ears. Yet carried by the surging waves of deep recognition—of who he truly was and who she discovered herself to be—she embraced her wandering and searching life. While the water jar sat abandoned at the well, she took possession of a new life. She could now proclaim with certainty what she knew to be her own truth. She discovered the relationship for which she had been searching.

FOR REFLECTION

What parts of my life have I isolated from the company of others? What prompted me to voluntarily withdraw and submerge those precious pieces of myself?

What is my heart tired of fighting? In what ways have I exhibited boldness as a result of this fatigue?

Where is the evidence that I possess enough courage and audacity within me to dialogue with the challenges in my life? What am I afraid I will discover in the process?

When will I allow the questions and Wisdom submerged in the depths of my heart to surge and bubble to the surface? How will I discern the authenticity of this inner knowing?

For what is my heart searching? How will I recognize the goal of my searching when I encounter it?

Serving at the Table

THE MOTHER-IN-LAW OF PETER

When Jesus entered Peter's house,
he saw his mother-in-law lying in bed with a fever;
he touched her hand, and the fever left her,
and she got up and began to serve him.

Matthew 8:14-15

As the matriarch of the household, she was entitled to her position of authority and so sat regally under the shade trees in the upper courtyard. From this vantage point she could oversee the activities of her extended family, suggest the manner in which to prepare foods to their best advantage, share Wisdom and consolation when necessary, and enjoy the laughter of her many grandchildren. Her face, lined and weathered by time, reflected the enduring quality of the distant mountains to all in her presence. On any given day, those who looked at her could also see in her smiling eyes the sparkling waves of the nearby sea. But despite the energy of her household and its youngest generation, her mind and heart would often drift quietly inward for long moments to memories and the whispers of the angels.

Her joy each day was to arise before the sun and begin preparations for the meal that would break the fasting of the night. In those solitary moments, with her hands busy at their task, every breath pronounced the name of God and she gave thanks for the blessings of her life: *Yahweh, be mindful of this daughter of Wisdom, whom you have graced with advancing age.* Having spoken the words of her prayer through the sound of her breath, she greeted each day with arms outstretched, welcoming to the table all who sheltered in her son-in-law's home and would be sent forth from the table that day to go about their business.

Recently, a man newly come to Capernaum from Nazareth had sought the sanctuary of her son-in-law's home. He was gentle and compassionate, a man of eloquence and Wisdom far beyond his years. Unafraid of public reproach, he spoke to all manner of people with deep respect. She sensed a powerful energy emanating from his person and wondered who among her household was aware of it. *Certainly my daughter's husband responds to this man's inner authority, as do the children, who all follow him about like flocks of birds hoping for breadcrumbs!*

The rhythms of the ensuing days afforded her the occasional pleasure of overhearing the newcomer's teachings; but even on days when her path did not cross that of the newcomer, there were always people around her who spoke of his ability to heal and who recalled the parables he shared in public. Located midway between the synagogue and the shore, her son-in-law's home was a natural gathering place, where friends and neighbors felt free to stop and share the latest good news.

One morning, she awoke feeling restless and unusually warm for the pre-dawn hour, aware that her body was stiff and sore. *Ah, I am feeling my years more than usual today. Why now, when the hour promises only more of the sun's heat and there is much to do to be ready for the others when they awaken?* She persisted with the meal preparations and welcomed everyone to the table as she always did. Once the repast was taken, however, she retired to her bed rather than to the shade of the courtyard. As the sun climbed higher into the sky, the heat seemed to concentrate in her body. Her fevered brow was damp with perspiration and yet she shivered with chill at the slightest movement of air in the still room. Her daughter came to her out of concern, having noticed her absence from the courtyard. Water was graciously offered and gratefully accepted. *Yet the hours pass and I am no better for it. I call upon you, my God! Let my breath be my prayer to return to life and the service of all who dwell in this house…Yahweh…Yahweh…Yahweh….*

She lapsed into half-sleep, only to be aroused moments later, or so it seemed, to the sounds of the men returning from synagogue. Voices drew closer and soon she heard footsteps at the threshold of the room. *My daughter arrives with water once again.* As her eyelids fluttered open, she discerned a shadowy presence close at hand. She deliberately willed her eyes to focus on the figure before her, only to be gripped with surprise as she did so. Bending close was the newcomer, the Teacher. A gentle smile crinkled the corners of his mouth, while above it his eyes were filled with deep knowing and compassion.

Astonished at his proximity, she lay still, unable to discern whether she should pull away from him or allow herself to be embraced by his tenderness. *Why does he come to me? What does he ask of me? Who am I that he should be mindful of an old woman?* While her mind and heart still raced, he reached out to touch her. He laid his hand upon hers, allowing it to linger with gentle pressure. He looked at her hand in such a way that she thought he saw every loaf of bread she had kneaded, cup of wine she had poured, drop of oil she had administered for healing, bucket of water she had drawn, and child she had held and comforted. *Yes, somehow he sees it all and blesses my humble work.* With this realization, she sensed a healing power flood her being. His eyes came back to her own with confirmation of the exchange of healing energy—and she smiled.

He withdrew his hand and pulled himself up to stand by her bedside, as if waiting for her response. She could still feel the warmth of his touch and swallowed the lump of fear that caught in her throat. Without further hesitation, she arose from her bed to face the Teacher. *Sir, you need food and drink after your time of prayer and teaching. Go to the courtyard, sit in the shade of my tree, and I will bring you refreshment!*

Inundated with the same joy she felt upon rising each day, she hurried to minister to the Teacher and his followers with the preparation of a small feast. The work of her hands and heart would express her gratitude for the privilege of continuing to serve in the way she was best able.

FOR REFLECTION

Why do I dismiss myself as too ordinary to possess qualities worth presenting to others? What prompts me to think this way?

What would help me to discern the gifts and talents I am best able to offer in service to the world? How must I reconfigure my daily routine in order to carve out the time necessary for this discernment?

What brings me deep joy and satisfaction in life? How do I go about acknowledging that this may be what I am authentically called to do in my life when it may be at odds with what is already known and secure?

In what way am I aware of my life's work as a ministry to the world; how might I affirm this within myself? To what degree is the respect and acknowledgement of others important to my ministering in the world?

What risks am I willing to take in order to bring my passions to light? What would cause me to rise to this occasion?

No Longer Invisible

THE WIFE OF THE FISHERMAN

Once while Jesus was standing beside the lake of Gennesaret and the crowd was pressing in on him to hear the word of God, he saw two boats there at the shore of the lake; the fishermen had gone out of them and were washing their nets. He got into one of the boats, the one belonging to Simon, and asked him to put out a little way from the shore. Then he sat down and taught the crowds from the boat. When he had finished speaking, he said to Simon, "Put out into the deep water and let down your nets for a catch."

When they had done this, they caught so many fish that their nets were beginning to break. So they signaled their partners in the other boat to come and help them. And they came and filled both boats, so that they began to sink.

Then Jesus said to Simon, "Do not be afraid; from now on you will be catching people." When they had brought their boats to shore, they left everything and followed him.

Luke 5:1-4, 6-7, 10b-11

It seemed to be the beginning of an ordinary day. Her husband left while darkness still enfolded the village. There were times when she resented his trade, which required him to leave their shared bed in the quiet hours before dawn. Today, however, a strange longing prompted her to follow him to the doorway of their home in silence and watch as he faded into the distance toward the beach. *May the Lord be gracious to you today, my Love.* Soon the plain would be visible—a sea of land to balance the waters—with its open fields, its columnar trees, and the mountains in the distance. Her spirit wandered for a few moments beyond the horizon, exploring what she imagined to exist beyond the threshold of her life. But the sound of footsteps drew her back. She knew the sounds well. She had listened to them every morning since her childhood, as her mother arose and gave praise to the Lord before setting about the chores she now knew so well herself. Yes, there was water to draw from the well and food to prepare, so she turned to go inside. *My husband is good and gracious. Lord, I give thanks for his generous protection of my widowed mother. May your gracious care fill his nets this day.*

She laughed and smiled to see the old woman moving about. *Was it only a few days ago that the prophet rebuked the fever that possessed her? Look at her now, preparing the meal that will break this night's fast!* While her hands were busy, the sun rose in the sky and its brightness now glinted off the lake waters like so many thousands of jewels as she went about her tasks. Pausing, she looked toward the beach where she expected to see the boats unloading their catch. She squinted in the bright light and realized suddenly that an unusual number of people were standing on the shore gesturing toward the water. Still out in deep water, her husband's boat and another were barely visible above the waterline. *No! It must not sink!* She could not make out the figure of her husband among those on board and, for an instant, could not feel the beat of her own heart.

Before she was conscious of it, her feet were carrying her quickly down the long path to the water's edge. *Surely, he is strong enough to swim to shore. Lord, do not take him from me!* Pushing through the crowd, she reached the shore just as the heavily laden boats arrived, and relief washed over her like refreshing rain. There he was talking with a man who, as she drew near, she recognized as the healing Prophet. Her husband's boat and another were filled with the largest catch she had ever seen! *God, you are generous today! I praise you for the livelihood you provide for my husband and for the food that graces our table!* Moving closer, she began to hear the words of their conversation. She approached them just as the Prophet, with an encouraging hand on her husband's shoulder, was telling him to fear not for he would be catching people from now on!

A confused smile appeared on her face. *What does he mean? How does a fisherman catch people?* Looking to her hard-working, practical husband, she hoped to hear from him some sense of what this meant. But as both men turned to her, what she saw was a look of acceptance and excitement on her husband's face, as if fishing for people was the most normal work in the world! She had seen this look before—on their wedding day, on the days when each of their children were born, and on the day he inherited his own father's boat. Suddenly, fear gripped her heart and blood rushed to her cheeks. *What are you doing? You have a family to care for and feed! You can't go fishing for people! What about these fish? Who will take them to the market? Who will mend the nets? Lord, do not take him from me!*

Met with the knowing look only a husband and wife are able to exchange, she then turned to the Prophet, this man called Jesus, hoping for some indication that this was all just nonsense. Instead, his eyes spoke of truth and gave no indication of rescinding the offer. There was also something else—an overwhelming sense of urgency, assurance, and power emanating from him. She felt it instantly, coursing through her being. Its presence within her seemed to silence the fear, drawing determination, confidence, and courage into that space where only a moment ago she had already imagined and anticipated her husband's absence. That space was filling with thoughts of her mother tending to the house and the children, while she turned her attention to the affairs of her husband's business. Watching these two men as they walked away from her down the shoreline, with the life-giving waters lapping at their feet, she knew that not only had the course of her beloved husband's life changed direction, but her own was irrevocably altered in that instant as well. Her service in the world would now be anything but ordinary.

FOR REFLECTION

What events have irrevocably altered the course of my life's direction? Did I choose these milestones or were they imposed on me?

Have I participated graciously or reluctantly in the changes that have molded the person I am today? What voices of resistance or resonance did I hear within myself at these times?

Am I visible to myself? To others? How have I been challenged to look at myself as "anything but ordinary"?

When have I experienced an overwhelming sense of urgency, assurance, or power coursing through my being? What was I prompted to do as a result?

What is the truth I see and hear in my life right now? How will I proceed from this point forward?

Disowned

MY MOTHER AND SISTERS

Then his mother and his brothers came; and standing outside, they sent to him and called him. A crowd was sitting around him; and they said to him, "Your mother and your brothers and sisters are outside, asking for you. And he replied, "Who are my mother and my brothers?" And looking at those who sat around him, he said, "Here are my mother and my brothers! Whoever does the will of God is my brother and sister and mother."

Mark 3:31-35

Their hope had always been that he would make his living in Nazareth. It was difficult to imagine how life in the small village would continue without his daily presence. His kindnesses would be missed, along with his laughter. Capernaum was not so far away, but it was not here. Questions surfaced in the hearts of his mother and sisters, some spoken aloud and others held in silence. *Why Capernaum? What does Capernaum possess that cannot be found here in Nazareth? Yes, even as a boy he wandered away from us, insisting that he had business to attend to; now he needs to call Capernaum home? How does he expect us to let him go?*

Yet, they could not hold on to him. Amid tearful farewells and promises of visits, he had walked away into a future they could not imagine. Slowly, as the days and weeks passed, word of the circumstances of his daily life came by way of distant family and acquaintances, traders and travelers. He had presented himself to his kinsman at the Jordan and then gone off into the wilderness, only to be seen some forty days later near the seashore. *What is the purpose of this itinerant lifestyle he has chosen? And what has compelled him to choose it?* These questions invaded the minds and hearts of those close to him. They heard he was known to teach within the imposing walls of the black basalt synagogue of Capernaum. There were rumors of his journeys to neighboring villages, as well as stories of the large crowds of people who surrounded him, even in his own home. His relatives were told of an intimate group of disciples who shadowed his every move. *Is this the very same son and brother who we watched playing in the mud as a child? The inquisitive one who was unashamed to ask how bread was made? The attentive one who conversed openly with us and valued the Wisdom traditions and insights of women? Yes, his open, accepting manner might be as attractive to others as it is to us, but how could strangers possibly understand him? He is known in this way only to us, only to those who love him.*

For some time, however, there had also been disturbing questions and accompanying accusations about their beloved son and brother. These were more difficult to reconcile within the hearts of his mother and sisters. It was said he ignored the Law. Accounts of healing those possessed with evil spirits reached their ears, and they heard he ate with tax collectors and sinners. There were spurious and scandalous tales told of blasphemy coming from his mouth and of argumentative engagements with the Pharisees and scribes. The people were saying, "He has gone out of his mind."

Worry weighed heavily in their every hushed conversation. Protective instincts surged within them and crashed against walls of their own sense of helplessness. *What can we do? There are those who will seize the opportunity to destroy him out of fear. May the Lord protect our precious son and brother!* Memories of the little boy at play in Egypt, safe from those who sought to kill him, flooded his mother's mind and heart. *He must come home to us, to the safety of our home and our care.* Frantic to ensure his well-being, plans were hurriedly made to travel to Capernaum—more than a day's journey away—under the protection of his brothers.

They followed the trade route and passed through the fishing village of Magdala. The sight of the Sea of Galilee encouraged their feet to move forward and heightened their anticipation of a reunion at last. But there was little on this journey to prepare them for what they were about to see and hear. As they approached his home, the crowds pressed in from all sides. People of every sort had made their way to this place and crowded the home's courtyard, straining to hear the contentious voices emanating from its center and, in turn, arguing among themselves in barely restrained voices. His mother and sisters exchanged confused and questioning looks. *What is happening? Is that his voice? Are you sure? Where is he? Help us, O God, to reach him! Why are there so many people here?* Jostled by the crowds, their forward progress was hampered despite the assistance of his brothers. The women's voices were drowned out and swallowed by the sheer numbers around them. Their faces went unrecognized and no accommodation was made for them as the family of the Teacher. Having reached the gate to the courtyard, they could go no farther. His mother, unable to stride boldly forward as she did many years ago in the Temple precincts, sent word to him through the crowd, asking for their presence be made known to her son.

Her message traveled to him as if carried on the gentle swells of the sea itself. One after another listened to the message and passed it along until, at last, it reached its intended recipient. Quiet ensued, with a hush that rippled backward in waves to the source of the message. As he stood, he looked back over the heads of the crowd sitting around him to find them. Expectant and hopeful, they anticipated that their son and brother would stride toward them, glad to behold them after so long an absence. He met their gazes and searched their faces one by one for what seemed to his mother and sisters to be fleeting, yet eternal moments. His countenance was open, but possessed of a quality they did not recognize. Turning from them to take in the crowd, he gestured as if to embrace all present and spoke with a clear, resonant voice: *Who are my mother and my brothers? Whoever does the will of God is my brother and sister and mother.*

Disowned. They stood in the midst of this unfamiliar village, struggling with emotions that surfaced unbidden. *No! It is true; he has lost his mind! This is not possible!* Unbelieving, indignant, possessive, afraid, defeated, hurt, angry…they found themselves once again embraced by his tender and imploring eyes. With strength and determination, his eyes begged for understanding and acceptance of the inclusive and unconventional life he had embarked upon.

Disowned. Mother and sisters were faced with an untenable choice and each struggled with it in her own way. *Have we lost him? How can we accept as family the strangers who we do not know? Why must we share the one our hearts love beyond measure? Why must we allow him to risk his own well-being? Are we to let go of him, or open the gates of our hearts even wider?*

Despite the inward maelstrom of questions, not one of the women walked away. At that moment, a new consciousness began to emerge among them. In the days to come they discovered that, by being "disowned," they were free to hold within themselves the dissonant questions that would eventually reshape their lives. These questions would allow them to challenge their perceptions of the world and to seek answers, no matter how unconventional. They were now free to remain at home or to follow the son and brother they loved. His love confronted them with the choice to risk the consequences of following their own convictions, as well as the opportunity to seek the Truth—whatever and wherever it might be.

FOR REFLECTION

What have I sought to control and protect in my own life? Why do I fear this aspect of my life—because of its fragility or because it has the potential to release my greatest expression of power?

In what ways am I possessive rather than expansive in my love? Is it possible for me to serve the world by remaining small?

Am I comfortable holding questions that have no ready answers? What feelings are evoked in me when I find myself existing in this in-between place?

How have I met the challenge of following my convictions and seeking truth in my own life? In what ways am I invigorated or daunted by the inevitable obstacles and consequences of this journey?

When truth does not match my perception of what should be, do I feel "disowned"? What qualities of resilience do I possess that would allow me to overcome this feeling of abandonment?

Word of Love

THE CENTURION'S SLAVE

After Jesus had finished all his sayings in the hearing of the people, he entered Capernaum. A centurion there had a slave whom he valued highly, and who was ill and close to death. When he heard about Jesus, he sent some Jewish elders to him, asking him to come and heal his slave. When they came to Jesus, they appealed to him earnestly, saying, "He is worthy of having you do this for him, for he loves our people, and it is he who built our synagogue for us." And Jesus went with them, but when he was not far from the house, the centurion sent friends to say to him, "Lord, do not trouble yourself, for I am not worthy to have you come under my roof; therefore I did not presume to come to you. But only speak the word, and let my servant be healed. For I am also a man set under authority, with soldiers under me; and I say to one, 'Go,' and he goes, and to another, 'Come,' and he comes, and to my slave, 'Do this,' and the slave does it." When Jesus heard this he was amazed at him, and turning to the crowd that followed him, he said, "I tell you, not even in Israel have I found such faith." When those who had been sent returned to the house, they found the slave in good health.

Luke 7:1-10

She was impressed those many years ago by his stature. His leadership and ability to command respect were well known among all in Capernaum, Roman and Jew alike. He had come to the edge of the Sea of Galilee, like so many others, to stamp the indelible mark of the Empire upon the landscape. Yet unlike any other, he uniquely altered the condition of her being.

Pressed into the service of his household, she had initially harbored fear and caution with regard to her new existence. *I am alone in this household, despite the many who surround me. Why does Yahweh allow this? Where is the safety of God's own arm?* The occupying forces imposed themselves upon her people with a threatening presence, and she knew that much depended on her—and others like her—to maintain what little gracious indulgence could be gained by their exacting servitude. Yet, had her family not experienced the tenuous poverty of their station in life, she might never have known the world that opened before her within the complexity and foreign traditions of the centurion's domestic confines.

It was a disciplined compound in which to live, yet it felt alive with displays of courage and skill. Despite her hesitancies, she found herself watching from the corners and shadows as the centurion exercised his mastery of military weapons and maneuvers, meted out discipline, and controlled the training of those in his command. Much to her own surprise and consternation, she grew to admire this man's abilities, as well as the compassion of his personal demeanor toward all who served under him. She observed what appeared to be restraint and justice at work in his even-handed authority.

For the first time in her life, she felt a stirring within herself that prompted her to utter the words of Solomon's great song. *My beloved is all radiant and ruddy, distinguished among ten thousand…his arms are rounded gold…his body is ivory work…his legs are alabaster columns….This is my beloved.* The strength of her feelings overwhelmed her. They belied the reality of the situation, yet she could not deny their effect, which she would now have to hide.

Early on, he noticed her lingering at the fringes of the household. Occasionally, he summoned her into the open courtyard to inquire as to her responsibilities that morning or to pluck a succulent fruit from her basket. His manner was courteous, with no hint of impropriety. As the days passed, she came to see him not as conquering overlord but as one who shared her own humanity. She witnessed his fatigue, his frustration, his hunger, and his quiet contemplation. She hardly noticed that he allowed her to see these private moments by calling specifically for her to tend to his needs and then gently commanding her to look into his eyes as he spoke to her. Gradually, the words of Solomon's song came again to her lips: *Turn away your eyes from me, for they overwhelm me!*

Each Sabbath, she was allowed to join her own people in prayer. Over time, in the conversations before and after prayer, she found it became more and more difficult to reconcile the resigned and sometimes bitter words of her people against the Roman occupation with this unique man she had gradually come to know. Indeed, her vision of him was justified by the tolerance and respect with which he received the elders of the community and in turn was received by them. This seemed an extraordinary exception to the rules of military engagement.

After many years, a quiet ease was born of their close proximity. Confidences were shared and small intimacies exchanged, all the while maintaining the decorum of their disparate positions. Yet without doubt, there existed a love between them that defied all the conventions of their impossible situation. Eventually, he had taken ownership of the land that was granted to him upon completion of his service and he dedicated his considerable pension to the building of a synagogue. It was her love, however, that had taken possession of him.

She understood that there could never be a formal acknowledgement of their relationship in the usual sense. Instead, there stood in public view a synagogue that had risen slowly over the years she had shared with him, built with foundation walls of black basalt. Gray marble columns and carefully cobbled floors adorned this edifice born of love. To some, it appeared that he loved the whole of her people, without any knowledge of the true impetus for his action. Their eyes do not see what stands before them in full view. *They are foolishly mistaken to think the foundation to be made only of stone.*

Despite its enduring devotion, however, their love was not impervious to the devastation of illness and imminent death. For all the power of his authority and strength, the time came when the centurion was helpless in the face of an unyielding illness that struck his beloved. *Look, his eyes betray him. If only I could reach out to smooth the crease of his brow and assure him of my love.* Just when the moment of utter heartbreak approached, this centurion—a man who knew the power of a single word on the battlefield—sought out the One from Capernaum who was known to heal by word alone, sending emissaries from the synagogue to implore the Healer that such a word be spoken over his beloved immediately. As he waited, keeping vigil over this servant who he valued more highly than any other, the centurion realized that death had begun to fight him for her life. Feeling unworthy in the face of this immense, desperate struggle with death, more messengers were dispatched to countermand the previous request with a new one: *Simply speak the word that mends the broken and restores the dying to life.*

Jesus was touched deeply by the power of this urgent request. He felt the energy of compassion resonate within his heart and leap beyond him to reinvigorate and enliven a love thought lost. The Love that had called the universe forth into being lured this beloved woman back from the edge of death. Surfacing into consciousness, she found herself held by the faithful gaze of the centurion. The words of the great song echoed within her heart yet again and joined with her own thoughts: *Do not stir up or awaken love until it is ready! I am coming up from the wilderness leaning upon my beloved. For love is strong as death, passion fierce as the grave.* In that moment, she found herself filled with a spirit of well-being and peace, which seemed to acknowledge that even her unconventional and humble love was worthy.

FOR REFLECTION

In what ways would the ground of my being shift if I allowed myself to see beyond the conventional and expected in life? How might I be lulled into complacency by a lack of imagination?

As I look into the myriad faces of humanity, where do I see reflections of my own face? What is my desire and capacity for seeking common ground with other people?

If I were to permit love to truly guide my actions and to possess me fully, what dimensions of myself would I retain? What elements of myself would I have to let go of?

What is in danger of dying because I refuse to acknowledge its place in my life? What level of urgency do I feel as I look at this piece of myself that is in danger of being lost?

How much am I willing to risk for the sake of love? Does the power of Divine Love resonate within me or do I shrink from engaging its immensity and responsibility?

Hope Deep Within

THE WIDOWED MOTHER OF NAIN

Soon afterwards he went to a town called Nain, and his disciples and a large crowd went with him.

As he approached the gate of the town, a man who had died was being carried out. He was his mother's only son, and she was a widow; and with her was a large crowd from the town.

When the Lord saw her, he had compassion for her and said to her, "Do not weep."

Then he came forward and touched the bier, and the bearers stood still. And he said, "Young man, I say to you, rise!"

The dead man sat up and began to speak, and Jesus gave him to his mother.

Luke 7:11-15

Desolation surrounded her on every side, hounded her every breath, taunted her with the realization that she did, in fact, still breathe. She felt as if she were simply a shell, cast aside and emptied of its living inhabitant. Where once energy and joy had existed, there were now the dismal prospects of solitude and poverty, hunger and uncertainty. Fear beat against the door of her heart, relentless and unwavering. *How will I live? Why must I go on? I have nothing. I am nothing. I am alone…I am alone…I am alone.*

For as long as her husband and son lived, she was sheltered by their love. Until the moments of their separate deaths, she knew with certainty who she was—a wife, a mother. *But now, who am I now? I am an unwelcome burden, a mouth to feed. The taste of alms will be bitter, yet what choice do I have? Perhaps I should lie down in my home—while I am yet able to call it mine—and wait for death to come for me, too.*

Despite the overwhelming temptation to surrender herself to the quietude of death, there still remained a strong pulse of motherhood within her body, which recognized that her son, even in death, needed her. She allowed no one else to wash his body or to swaddle him in his burial shroud. While occupied by the necessities of death, memories flooded over her and carried her upon their waves in exact imitation of the waters of the sea, as they push and pull at an empty shell left on the sand. She allowed herself to be tossed and turned across the sands of time, comforted by the scriptural admonition: *Do not forget.* She worried, as a mother would, about not going ahead of her son to prepare the way. *Where has the light of his smile gone? Will he know my love in this new place?* Tenderness flowed from her hands, the expression of some infinitesimally small but present piece of her that determined silently to do what she could, for as long as she could, for this child of her womb. Until the tomb was sealed, she was yet a mother. Defying the Law and succumbing instinctively only to love, she kissed his brow gently, just as she had so many times in the past, and caressed his cheek. Her eyes tried desperately to take in every detail before she covered his face, murmuring gentle reassurances to her son that all would be well. *If only I could truly believe this for myself.*

She completed her ritual by slowly cleansing her body three times with cool, clear water as she contemplated both the near and distant future. *Once I have finished with these ablutions, my son's body will be carried upon waves of lamentation and wailing to the tomb of my husband. I will undertake the journey once again, recalling and resisting every step on the way. And, when it is my time, who will prepare my body and journey with it? Who will bring me home to my husband and son?*

With tears of salt welling in her eyes, she turned to the doorway and indicated all was ready—everything with the exception of her heart. All that could be done now was to simply hold him with her eyes and carry him with her spirit. The mourners moved toward the southern edge of the village, where they would start the ascent up the slope of the hill of Moreh to the place where tombs were cut into the rock. Not conscious of her surroundings, she stumbled on the rough ground and had momentary cause to glance behind the procession to where Mount Tabor stood in silent witness to her grief. *Look how its shape protrudes from the earth like a mother's breast. My son will be received back into a mother's womb; I am grateful to you, O God, for this small comfort.*

Turning to begin her upward climb, her eyes beheld another procession—although this one did not seem to have the same purpose. Populated by an assortment of people, the man leading them commanded her attention. *Who is this and why does he approach? I am certain he is a stranger to me, but his face appears troubled and full of sorrow.* The atmosphere on the hillside was charged with an uncertain energy that caused all those in the burial procession to stop. Without hesitation, this leader moved to stand near her and looked deeply into her eyes, past the tears, into her fluid depths. His look transformed instantly to one of great empathy and compassion. She felt something shift inside of herself, almost as if a sluice gate lifted open and upset the delicate balance of her emotions in a powerful rush. Curiously, it did not plunge her into even greater depths of grief; rather, it felt as if she were buoyed to the surface of the murky depths within her, allowed once more to gasp and take in the air she thought had fled when death appeared. Another woman's son stood before her. She saw clearly his desire to remove the pain she felt at this moment, as well as his intention to allow hope to surge once again through her veins.

Do not weep. The tone of his utterance immediately silenced her crying and she drew a deep, expectant breath. This man, obviously a Teacher, moved to the bier upon which the body of her son lay and touched it—as intentionally and gently as if they were brothers. The words that flowed from his mouth in the next instant were startling in contrast, like cold water thrown in her face: *Young man, I say to you, rise!*

She felt herself caught in the space between breaths, suspended and drifting between opposite poles of reality. *Yes!… No!…How?…What are you doing?…This is impossible!…Who are you?…Can you really do this? O God, please…please!* A wellspring of hope burst forth from her to the surface of consciousness. She watched as her son's body came slowly back from Sheol—mesmerized by the rise and fall of his chest, the barely discernable twitches of stiff muscles and the audible signs of panic, bound as he was in the long, winding strips of burial cloth.

Maternal instinct and hope besieged the hesitancy and fear that lingered at the edges of her conscious awareness. *I must release him from these grasping bands! O God, you are gracious beyond all knowing!* Her hands worked deftly and quickly, even as she glanced furtively at the Teacher, who stood nearby watching her progress. When the last restraint dropped from her son's body and as she was overcome by emotion, she embraced this grown child of her womb as if for the first time. *My son and I are born again into the world. We live!* Turning to the Teacher, she saw him looking at a woman who stood nearby with an expression she recognized. It was the silent speech of a mother and son. As if he felt the weight of her gaze upon him, the Teacher turned, inclined his head slightly, and lifted his hand toward her reclaimed son in a gracious gesture. Likewise, she bowed in gratitude for his gift and reverenced the powerful energy she was privileged to experience. Her response was not due solely to the return of her son and her own restored welfare; instead, it was acknowledgement of the deep, indwelling trust and hope that re-opened to the surprising and mysterious work of God.

Even if death should visit again, desolation would be held at bay. Her previously unrecognized, internal power was revealed to her—an enduring resiliency in the face of life's worst storms and an immense capacity to float on the waves of deep hope.

FOR REFLECTION

Do I recognize the truth of my identity or do I allow myself to be defined primarily by the roles and relationships in my life? How can I affirm and give greater expression to this authentic core of my being that is undefined by those around me?

Does the future inspire fear or hope in my heart? What prompts this response in me?

In the face of significant losses, when did I feel desolation creeping in to my mind and heart? How did I respond? What have I learned in those experiences?

What signs exist that deep, indwelling trust and hope might reside within me? In what ways do I perceive myself as resilient in my approach to life?

What is dead inside me? What new life would I like to see brought forth from these dead places? How is it possible to open myself to the surprising and mysterious work of God?

Confidence

THE WOMAN OF EXTRAVAGANT LOVE

Then turning toward the woman, he said to Simon, "Do you see this woman? I entered your house; you gave me no water for my feet, but she has bathed my feet with her tears and dried them with her hair. You gave me no kiss, but from the time I came in she has not stopped kissing my feet. You did not anoint my head with oil, but she has anointed my feet with ointment. Therefore, I tell you, her sins, which were many, have been forgiven: hence she has shown great love…

Then he said to her, "Your sins are forgiven…Your faith has saved you; go in peace."

Luke 7:44-48, 50

She heard his teachings over the course of many weeks. The Teacher spoke at length of feasting and fasting, hungers and needs, of saving and destroying, blessings and woes, of forgiveness and love. As she listened and watched, she discovered his compassion reached into all levels of society without preconception or judgment. Wisdom allowed him to see humanity clearly and without contempt. He met people in the midst of illness or grief and saw deep beneath their public facades to the individual human beings who desired wholeness and healing. Gradually, she became aware that he drew upon a great reservoir of love and life-giving energy that, to her, seemed limitless. *Only the Creator would possess such unimaginable gifts… to be given without regard for cost or repayment. In the beginning, it was the Creator who blessed all of life and pronounced it good, established covenants that promised life. How could these be rescinded? The Teacher seems to draw upon God's life and covenant promises without effort, as easily as he draws breath…*

For days, she considered whether she ever thought of herself as party to the covenant with the Creator—whether or not she lived and drew breath from that unique relationship. *Are women included in the covenant relationship? We must be; the covenant would have been impossible without our foremother, Sarah. Yahweh pursued our people in love, and found favor with the women who have gone before me, blessing them with the children who would outnumber the stars of the heavens and the sands of the earth. But am I worthy?*

She existed with the assumption that her worthiness had been diminished over the course of her life, eroded by circumstances that affected her dignity and integrity—such as a woman could hope to possess. *Yet, I have never forgotten the Source of Life. Certainly, God embraced and honored women like Tamar, Bathsheba, Judith, Esther, and Ruth despite their deceit and trickery, murder and indiscretion. How am I so very different from them?*

Am I unworthy of God's hesed? How can I be less deserving of God's fierce loyalty granted through the covenant of love—even if my memory is not preserved, like that of my foremothers, for the generations to come? Would God love me less? Quietly, in the solitude of her being, she realized that she was beloved of God. Despite all that transpired within and beyond her control, the power of God's love could still reach into her depths.

And from those depths came an unbidden stream of tears, gratitude flowing forth. Knowing herself to be loved, she was filled with trust in the truth of God's reliable compassion and loyalty and the need to reciprocate this love. She glanced around at the wealth of her material possessions, searching for something that would reflect the light and beauty she felt in the moment. As her eyes came to rest on a delicate vessel of ointment, the heart within her breast moved her to great urgency. Grasping this small container, she found herself walking with assurance toward the house of the Pharisee Simon—where she knew the Teacher to be a guest—drawn onward as surely as a river being pulled to the sea by an unquestionable need to empty itself into something far greater.

Confident now of not being separated from God, but held instead with the unwavering fidelity of covenant love, she merged with the assembly of guests and servants and moved to where the Teacher reclined at table. Standing there, she felt for a moment as if she was transparent. Some of those present would see and judge her for what she lacked. But, this hardly mattered any longer. Self-assured, her grateful love flowed out to the Teacher through her tears, her touch, and her anointing. Engulfed by her ministrations, she neither heard words nor saw any gesticulations regarding her uninvited presence at table.

Do you see this woman?

The silence provoked by the Teacher's question startled her into attentiveness to what was happening around her. The

Teacher fixed his gaze upon her, recognition and compassion emanating from gentle eyes. Emboldened, she looked around the room into the faces of those considering the Teacher's inquiry. *Do they truly see me? Do they even want to see me? What do they see? Can their hearts melt enough to see beyond what they assume to know about me? But, more importantly, do I see each of them?* Consumed with the diversion of her own queries, there was only a vague sense in her that the Teacher continued speaking. While he spoke, however, her eyes came to rest on Simon the Pharisee, who very slowly took on the appearance of one humbled and chastised. She turned back once more to the Teacher, only to find him waiting for her.

His words confirmed what she already knew: *I am invited into covenant relationship. I am invited to approach with confidence for I am the beloved daughter of the Creator. I am loved endlessly, beyond limitation and imperfection. The Anointed One, the One who I trust, responds with faithful assurance that I am seen and cherished. My grateful heart knows the peace of this.*

FOR REFLECTION

*In what ways am I invited into mutual relationship
with the Divine? Is there something that motivates me
to live and draw breath in conscious awareness of this
relationship with my Creator God?*

*When have I questioned my worthiness to be loved
so limitlessly by God? How have I allowed the
circumstances of my life to diminish or erode my dignity
and integrity?*

*What convinces or challenges me to believe that I am
the beloved of the Creator? How can I encourage myself
to realize that I am known and created by the Divine as
an expression of deep, beautiful love?*

*How do I give expression to the inner urge to empty
myself into something far greater? What will distinguish
my genuine and true need for relationship from mere
self-gratification?*

*What circumstances would cause me to worry that
God's love will overwhelm and change how I exist in the
world? Under what conditions am I confident and self-
assured when I approach the energy of God's love?*

Reborn
to Womanhood

THE DAUGHTER OF JAIRUS

Just then there came a man named Jairus, a leader of the synagogue. He fell at Jesus' feet and begged him to come to his house, for he had an only daughter, about twelve years old, who was dying…

While Jesus was still speaking, someone came from the leader's house to say, "Your daughter is dead; do not trouble the teacher any longer."

When Jesus heard this, he replied, "Do not fear. Only believe, and she will be saved."

When he came to the house, he did not allow anyone to enter with him, except Peter, John and James, and the child's father and mother. They were all weeping and wailing for her; but he said, "Do not weep; for she is not dead but sleeping."

And they laughed at him, knowing that she was dead. But he took her by the hand and called out, "Child, get up!"

Her spirit returned, and she got up at once.

Luke 8:40-42, 49-55a

Over the course of her childhood, she watched excitedly each week from her place among the women as her father stood and called forth a teacher from all those present in the synagogue. She loved the stories and the tales woven around and through the instruction about the Scriptures; but the stories of her foremothers—although few—especially captivated her imagination. She longed to be a woman like Rebekah, Leah or Rachel who gave birth to nations. She yearned for the wisdom of Deborah and the courage of Jael. She desired the fidelity of Ruth and the beauty of Bathsheba, formerly the wife of Uriah. She wished for the cunning audacity of women such as Tamar and Rahab, who insisted on justice and loyalty. She wanted the strong and trusting heart of Hannah. *This is the woman I will be. I will be a matriarch as were these women before me!* Here in Capernaum, though, life was ordinary and at times even peaceful despite the Roman forces that occupied the land. On occasion, she caught small glimpses of these virtues in her mother's eyes and demeanor, but they disappeared quickly in the face of daily tasks. It was evident that she was destined for a much smaller role in the life of her people.

On a Sabbath not so long ago, an unusual Teacher from Nazareth came to her father's synagogue. He spoke with authority and many were astonished. As she listened, hoping to hear one of her beloved stories, a man cried out in a loud voice challenging the Teacher. Immediately, she heard the Teacher's commanding voice and the gasps of the assembly. Her mother reached for her and drew her near. *What has happened? Why are people whispering? Who is that man on the floor? Tell me, Mother! I am not so little any longer that you must shield me!* Without benefit of answers, she was shepherded out of the synagogue and onto the path that led to their home.

Weeks passed and the daily household tasks alongside her mother consumed her attention. There seemed to be less and less time for wandering and day-dreaming. Instead, her dreams became more practical. It was important now to learn the details of running a home. *Soon I will have a home of my own and a husband!* She noticed the changes within that began to mold her small frame into a shape more like her mother's. She knew the cycles of the moon would soon exert a power over her body she could not defy. It would not be long before she would join the other women in their time apart and the cleansing rituals that returned them to the embrace of their loved ones. The mystery of this glowed within her and quickened her step.

It was this sensation of change that, at first, masked the illness, which would soon overtake her feeling of well-being. At first, she accepted the discomforts of it with a determined will and a heart that desired to be strong and unafraid. Yet, questions persisted in her mind. *What is this poison that courses through me? Why have I not noticed the other women fighting this? How is it that they continue in their work? Is this what I must endure in order to fulfill my role in life?*

Gradually her hands weakened and her breathing became labored. She felt the burning of the midday sun within and shivered as the night's chill seemed to envelope her body. She felt the little girl who she was trying to leave behind reemerge, as she looked to her mother and father for reassurance and comfort. They were standing at the doorway of their home, and as she attempted to walk to them, she stumbled. She called to them, but the words did not escape her throat. Falling to the floor, the sunlight outside the door dissolved into darkness for her.

Time ceased to exist as the fever ravaged her. In the few wakeful moments she knew, she heard whispers and saw faces both of hope and resignation. Once, she heard her mother's voice desperately urging her father to find the Teacher who, only weeks before, healed a man in the synagogue. Then, she felt the darkness approaching once more and she gave herself to it, unable to summon the strength and courage of her foremothers to vanquish it.

It was impossible to know how much time had passed when, finally, her darkness began to recede. In its place, her ears filled with the wailing of the mourners outside. Her mind began to clear. *What has happened? Who has died?* Opening her eyes to the light, she was greeted by the smiling visage of the Teacher. He touched her hand gently and spoke simply: *Child, get up.* As she repeated these words to herself, there arose from a place deep within a new energy, emerging slowly as if her child-self was leading a new person by the hand into the world. It was the nascent woman, not the child, who stood up to face the Teacher—the person of potential and creative power, the one who would bring goodness and compassion into the world through her power to love. Facing the Teacher, she understood at last what had moved the women of generations past and she felt the promise of faith and trust in God. It was as if she was born again.

FOR REFLECTION

What hopes and dreams have sustained me through my life's journey? If faced with the prospect of relinquishing a cherished dream, how do I imagine myself responding?

Who are my role models? What qualities do they possess that I desire to assimilate? What reflections of myself do I see in them?

Do I respond to change in my life with resistance and confusion or do I allow myself to be vulnerable and malleable as the forces of transition engage me in becoming more authentic? In what way do I exercise my free will in choosing one or the other of these responses?

At what point(s) in life did I feel my authentic nature assert itself and emerge from within? What emotions were evoked in me by these experiences?

If change is inevitable in life, what has the process of rebirth propelled me toward? As a result of the waxing and waning pressures of this movement, what has unfolded within me?

Audacity

THE HEMORRHAGING WOMAN

Now there was a woman who had been suffering from hemorrhages for twelve years. She had endured much under many physicians, and had spent all that she had; and she was no better, but rather grew worse.

She had heard about Jesus, and came up behind him in the crowd and touched his cloak, for she said, "If I but touch his clothes, I will be made well."

Immediately her hemorrhage stopped; and she felt in her body that she was healed of her disease.

Immediately aware that power had gone forth from him, Jesus turned about in the crowd and said, "Who touched my clothes?"

And his disciples said to him, "You see the crowd pressing in on you; how can you say, 'Who touched me?'"

He looked all round to see who had done it. But the woman, knowing what had happened to her, came in fear and trembling, fell down before him, and told him the whole truth.

He said to her, "Daughter, your faith has made you well; go in peace, and be healed of your disease."

Mark 5:25-34

Joy and suffering entered her life simultaneously twelve years ago. The birth of her daughter was the advent of a physical condition that rent the very fabric of her life. Her thoughts often drifted back to that day and she could recall the anticipation, the struggle to bring forth new life, the overwhelming elation when the infant appeared whole and beautiful—and the panic of the midwives when they could not stem the flow of blood that followed her child into the world. The women ministered to her with great tenderness over the ensuing days, but they were unsuccessful in their attempts to stop her bleeding entirely. She felt weak and fatigued. Nursing the child sapped every ounce of her energy and strength.

As time passed, her flow of blood slowed, but never subsided. It appeared unbidden in her mouth and nose; it welled under the surface of her skin and was expelled with her bodily functions. The joints of her body became swollen and distended with pooled blood, only to be replaced by stiffness and pain whenever the pooling receded; it was a constant cycle, more insistent and all-encompassing than any known by the women of her family. Her body gradually became contorted and disfigured; it imprisoned her in years of isolation and banishment. To leave her home even for the most ordinary of purposes, she risked personal embarrassment and defiled all who came in contact with her. There were no spontaneous visits to the well or the market place. The people of Capernaum came to know her ailment and avoided every possibility of meeting her. Her own husband, while he still lived, withdrew from her. Save for the daughter who saw past the bodily deformity and loved her mother unconditionally, she was bereft of relationship and community. Yet soon, even her daughter, who was approaching marriageable age, would necessarily abandon her for a husband and home of her own.

Pain and desperation drove her to seek relief and cure for

her malady. Among all the neighboring peoples, she sought out the physicians and healers who proffered remedies and hope. Everything she possessed was expended in this search—the meager household left after her husband's death, her integrity, her bonds of faith, and her own ebbing energy. Yet, her search revealed only the charlatans and the tricksters, those with promises that far exceeded their abilities to heal. She was the worse for their inept methods, which abetted the unrelenting progression of the disease that continued to ravage her frail body. She bore these ordeals with patient persistence, certain her search for true healing would lead her to renewed life. For this, she was willing to hemorrhage everything.

In a village such as Capernaum—full of fishermen and rabbis, soldiers and traders, bakers and servants—it was never difficult to learn the latest news if eyes and ears were kept open, even if all one could do was hover near a window or threshold. In exactly this manner, she heard of the Nazarene Healer who now made his home in her village. His compassion for the sick, the poor and the outcasts was apparently well known, and tales abounded about those he relieved of their burdensome conditions. Hearing this, myriad thoughts swirled through her mind and feelings engulfed her heart. *He will not be difficult to find. The people will crowd around him to see for themselves if the stories are true.*

And so, her unrelenting search for renewed life brought her to the edge of the crowd gathered around him that day. She caught small glimpses of him and snatches of his voice, enough to entice her to approach more closely despite the pressing numbers in the throng. *Why do I risk being seen? How foolish of me! Yet, I have no choice. All else has failed. I must be bold in order to heal myself. I choose life! If I but reach out and touch the fringe of his garment, will that be enough?*

The crowd shifted and moved as one, just as fish in the sea

or birds in the air. As it did, she found herself within an arm's length of the Healer. *Now! I must touch the hem of his cloak now!* Within the space of a heartbeat, she reached out for healing and was swallowed once again by the mass of humanity surrounding her. Unsure of what had just transpired, she realized her heart was pounding as she willed herself to be invisible. Retribution for her audacity would come swiftly if she had been noticed. Despite the fear coursing through her, she felt the retreat of pain from her body. Glancing quickly at her hands, it was apparent her body was still contorted and bruised. There was no obvious evidence of healing that would allow someone to accuse her of violation.

Who has touched me? His voice held the tone of one pleading at the loss of something precious. A chorus of other voices responded in surprise and dismissal, reminding him of the impossibility of knowing the touch of one among so many in close proximity. She could see him searching the faces of all those around him, and his own face revealed something she knew all too well—he felt the hemorrhage of life as it flowed from him. *See, he is deeply aware of his flow of life and he is searching the crowd to discover if anyone else has noticed!* His gaze fell upon her and they recognized one another as the source and receptacle of the power that crossed between them, hemorrhaging and healing simultaneously. A compelling, pulsing energy united them in that moment and, intensely self-conscious, she moved forward in awe and reverence of its mystery.

What spilled forth from her now was not blood, but the deliberate release of the whole truth—her desires for relief, peace, community, relationship, reentry into society. *Your journey of conviction and persistent searching has brought you to this moment of healing. You have stretched out your hand and touched the mystery of life itself, Daughter.* As his words echoed in her heart, she realized his forceful hemorrhage birthed her anew into the world. The cord that had entwined her body and restrained her spirit was severed and she took her first breath.

FOR REFLECTION

What causes the hemorrhaging of life for me or the depletion of my energy? How is my relationship with the community of Creation impaired as a consequence of this diminishment?

In the face of challenges that could potentially distort my life, what part of me wants to simply sink into helplessness? What part of me resists that urge? Which is the stronger response?

What is my capacity, regardless of cost or discomfort, for searching out solutions to the unexpected and unwelcome dimensions of my life? From where does this capacity originate?

How deep is my desire to reach for what is life-giving when faced with the risk of personal embarrassment or possible retribution at the hand of another? Is it my fear or my desire that is stronger?

Does the vulnerable openness needed to receive healing energy create a welcome, expansive space within me or am I immobilized by the unknown possibilities that stretch before me? By what means can I develop a balanced approach to openness and healing?

Given Voice

THE HEALING OF THE ONE WHO WAS MUTE

After they had gone away,
a demoniac who was mute was brought to him.

And when the demon had been cast out,
the one who had been mute spoke;
and the crowds were amazed and said,
"Never has anything like this been seen in Israel."

Matthew 9:32-33

The sound of her own voice delighted her as a little girl. She laughed and shrieked at play, and allowed the wind to carry her voice down to the sea. She sang the songs and hymns her mother taught her while they prepared meals or mended clothes. Her bright and observant mind found so much to talk about with whomever she met, and the market provided endless reasons to ask questions. It was not unheard of back then for her father to plead with her for just a few moments of silence in order to conduct business or to recite a short prayer.

She respected her mother's voice and knew how her mother wielded influence in their home with various tones and inflections. Without question, she understood her mother's intentions by her choice of words. *When will I be listened to in that manner? When will my words and their meaning cause others to take notice?* Impatience stirred within her for a voice of authority like her mother's, a voice that could teach and console, urge and direct, or chide and correct. *I have only a little voice now, but someday…* Her little words often drifted into big dreams.

As she grew, she learned when it was appropriate for a woman to speak—and where. She listened carefully to the unspoken messages of the proverbs, which likened a contentious woman's voice to the continual dripping of a rainy day. She was aware that a loud woman was considered foolish and ignorant—the last thing she ever wanted to be. *No! My voice will be respected. I will be known for my Wisdom.* As the result of her determination, she became skilled at listening and observing. She was intrigued by the conversations of the old women who gathered in shaded courtyards and she hung onto every word uttered by the women who came to the well each morning. Her heart grasped every morsel of experience and knowledge that could be gleaned from those older than she.

The time of her womanhood approached and with it came dreams that were more real and intense than anything she had previously known. She envisioned a husband and children, and she heard her own voice calling to them. She often awoke from her sleep with the sense that the power of her voice was respected in the dream, not only by her family, but by merchants and neighbors who consulted her on a variety of matters. In the daytime hours, she considered what the lives of the prophets Miriam, Deborah, Huldah, and Noadiah had been like. Stories of the prophet Anna came to her mind, as well. She wondered how all of these women could speak the message of God. *Certainly, I must open my heart to the Lord, just as they did, and listen carefully for God's word to speak to me. Yet, will anyone listen to me? Or, will they ignore my witness and dismiss me as insignificant?*

Days and months passed without note, one much the same as another. She continued to listen and to observe the world around her with rapt attention, absorbing everything in the manner of a dry cloth dipped in water. It was a struggle to quiet her heart, so as to hear God's word when it might be spoken—her own voice often bubbled to the surface unbidden and filled the home where she and her mother worked side by side. It was not uncommon to retire at the end of the day worn and weary, yet even then she found voice to offer praise and thanks to God.

One morning, upon waking, she realized an unseen force constricted her throat and, though terrified, she could not call out. *What power grips my voice and silences it? What demon invaded my sleep to deprive me of my voice—and why?* Over the course of days and weeks, remedies were sought. She drank wine with honey and soothing herbs, but to little avail. Furious with her inability to speak, she felt maddened by the words that welled up inside her. Attempts at speech came out like the unintelligible groanings of an animal. Even a self-imposed silence to comfort her throat only inflamed her temper and caused her to lash out in unrestrained horror at the prospect of not being able to communicate. Attempts to make her will known were misunderstood by even those who loved her. Gestures became wildly articulated; she was prevented from speaking as days, then weeks, passed. Many in Capernaum began to whisper and avoid her, assuming her condition was indeed the work of a demon, or perhaps of an unclean spirit known to associate with women who had sinned. *I can hear you, you fools! Your compassion is required, not your condemnation!* The desire to vindicate herself only provoked her to greater outbursts. She was trapped within the confines of her own mind and body, helpless.

Without voice, she was not free. Lacking the power of speech, she knew even the meager authority a woman could expect to exert was stripped from her, as well as the hope of speaking God's word. Deep within her heart, she knew now that she possessed a Wisdom earned through experience and careful attention that would remain unspoken in this persistent condition. The seeming futility of her dreams and desires fueled her present vacillation between despair and rage. *Even if God should speak to me, I am not free to give voice in response to God's word. I am nothing now!* The deadening silence enveloped her spirit and fed the seething rage within her breast.

Months passed. Unable to understand or placate her distress, family members heard of healings that took place nearby where the paralyzed walked and the sick were made well. Deciding to risk public humiliation and embarrassment, their love urged her to seek out the Healer. A glimmer of hope arose within her heart and she allowed herself to be led out into the street. It was not long before their little party met with a crowd moving slowly toward them, led by two who they had known to be blind, but who now were proclaiming the release from their infirmity. Following close behind was the Healer, a native of Capernaum known as Jesus. Filled with wild expectation, she approached him and parted the attending crowd, which drew back in fear of her obvious possession.

Jesus did not recoil. He stood before her in gentle, patient anticipation and rapt attention. With low, murmured words, Jesus reached out to touch her. In the space of a heartbeat, a sense of warmth and peace suffused her and the constriction that had become her constant companion dissipated. The anxiety and panic that held her voice captive relaxed its grip and released the stranglehold over her disturbed body. Her untamed gesturing subsided into arms resting at her side. Jesus' face broke into a broad smile and he inquired about whether she had anything to tell him. She opened her mouth hesitantly, only to discover that once more words bubbled forth from the stream that had never ceased to flow deep within, leaving the crowd agape around her. Wonder and awe overwhelmed her. In that instant, she realized, despite the cautionary language of the Law, that her woman's voice was judged as valuable and worthy of being restored. *I am free now to tell of God's goodness and mercy in my life! God's own Word has healed me.* In the first moments of her new awareness, words describing this precious gift filled her mouth and spilled into the ears of those surrounding her. *My voice will honor and reverence God for the rest of my days.*

FOR REFLECTION

Have I known periods in my life when my voice has been muted by forces outside myself? If asked to describe how I felt at these times, how would I characterize my response to being subdued?

How do I respond when my words are strangled and I am at a loss to communicate my thoughts and desires? What alternate means are at my disposal to articulate what I cannot readily speak out loud?

What circumstances exist within my life, right now, which feel as if they prevent me from freely speaking my mind and heart? Do these circumstances actually prevent me from using my voice or does my perception of the situation inhibit me in some way?

Do I feel absolutely silenced in any aspect of my life? How have I resisted or acquiesced to whomever or whatever has imposed this on me?

If given the dignity and power of my full voice, what would I feel compelled to say? Is there anyone in particular to whom I would speak?

Journey Home

THE SYRO-PHOENICIAN WOMAN

From there he set out and went away to the region of Tyre. He entered a house and did not want anyone to know he was there.

Yet he could not escape notice, but a woman whose little daughter had an unclean spirit immediately heard about him, and she came and bowed at his feet.

Now the woman was a Gentile, of Syro-Phoenician origin.

She begged him to cast the demon out of her daughter. He said to her, "Let the children be fed first, for it is not fair to take the children's food and throw it to the dogs."

But she answered him, "Sir, even the dogs under the table eat the children's crumbs."

Then he said to her, "For saying that, you may go—the demon has left your daughter."

So she went home, found the child lying on the bed, and the demon gone.

Mark 7:24-30

The sun sparkled on the dancing waves of the sea. Salt perfumed the mild breezes that swept over the city and gently caressed her skin. From the time when she was a little girl, standing then as she did now on the temple mount, she often imagined the city of Tyre as a pearl in the necklace of coastal isles strung along a curving arc across the waters. In the manner of the Lady of the Sea, the Great Goddess Astarte, Tyre opened her twin harbors like the loving arms of a mother to embrace the children of the world. *Yes, the arms of a mother. I know what it is to gather a child into my arms, my own precious daughter.* Recalling the delicate, slumbering form she so recently held, it was effortless to envision the Evening Star gazing from the heavens with love for those who honored her. A daughter was to be treasured, for through her the generations yet unborn would continue to know the depths of Divine Wisdom.

Her journey to the temple of Astarte, however, was born of urgent necessity this day. She would offer incense to the Mistress of the Heavens, imploring the Goddess for health and healing on behalf of her daughter, and thus her daughter's daughters. The child—whose skin was as pure and lustrous as the glass vessels of the Phoenician people—was held in the grip of an illness that would not relent, as though a demon sought to wrest from this little one the promise of tomorrow. With a mother's conviction, each step she took helped to frame her thoughts with clarity and to articulate her request with the profound simplicity and depth of a parent's love. The Wisdom of both her woman's body and her heart recognized all life as sacred. She knew the threads of life were woven with great intricacy and care, given pattern and texture, by the lives of all who honored Divine Wisdom. It was a deeper awareness, though, that informed her of the process by which Wisdom, in turn, bound together those who acted with compassion for one another.

Detaching her gaze from the expanse of waters before her,

she turned and entered the temple. With solemn gesture and silent supplication she invoked the protection of Astarte as the swirling and spiraling smoke lifted her desire to the Great Goddess. *She of the Womb, hear the prayer of this mother who begs for the life of her daughter. Allow your waters of life to flow over my child. Restore her with your own vitality.* Her prayer spoken, she listened with every fiber of her being for the response she felt sure would come. Yet, only silence entered her body and filled her. She strained with attention, but heard nothing. No sign appeared to comfort her with the assurance of Astarte's compassion. *How have I displeased you? Do you not find favor in my daughter? I await your word!* Eventually, with slow and tentative resignation, she arose and walked out of the temple precincts, passing the sacred cypress trees, confused and confounded by the silence.

Her mind wandered on the journey home, her distraction causing her to be jostled by the variety of people who crowded the markets and narrow lanes of Tyre. After a while, she looked into the faces around her. She knew some came seeking opportunities for trade, others the restorative quality of the sea and its shore. *By whatever name the Great Mother is called, all people rely upon She who gives life and shares the Wisdom of its sacredness with the people of the world. The Greeks call upon Sophia… while the Romans invoke Minerva…Egyptians worship Isis…and, the Jews know Yahweh's Hokmah. I beg to hear the compassionate voice of Divine Wisdom…*

In the midst of these thoughts, she was caught in the net of a few words overheard by chance. Several people in the street observed a small entourage quietly entering a house nearby. The travelers had entered Tyre from the direction of the mainland—Jews by their dress. One merchant spoke with certainty of having recognized a healer in their midst, a man known far and wide for his great Wisdom and compassion. Compelled by something beyond her will, she moved quickly to the house in question and entered as if one of the household. It took only moments before she met a man whose countenance, although fatigued, was rich in attention and awareness. Her heart, leaping before her, knew him to be the One whom she sought. Bowing deeply, with reverence for the powerful Wisdom she sensed emanating from him, she felt hope rise in the very center of her being. She also hoped Wisdom would be compassionate in every guise.

Unbidden, an urgent stream of words poured from her mouth. And indeed, it was Wisdom who answered her with a shrewd retort, demanding engagement and philosophical dialectic. *Let the children be fed first, for it is not fair to take the children's food and throw it to the dogs.* Aware that an appropriate response was critical, she chose her words with care, replying in Wisdom's own language. *Sir, even the dogs under the table eat the children's crumbs.* Surprise, respect, mirth and compassion mingled on the Healer's face. The look he returned to her was the very essence of Wisdom greeting Wisdom with powerful recognition.

Wholeness erupted into the world with its healing grace. A palpable energy flowed through her as she listened to his words: *For saying that, you may go—the demon has left your daughter.* The One who gives life, Divine Wisdom, spoke clearly to her in the unexpected voice of the Healer. The very power that extends beyond the farthest reaches of what any human understands honored her desire by acknowledging the pervasive, resonate vibration of Wisdom within her.

Speaking with the authority of Divine Wisdom, he had not put forth any conditions that required her to change or conform. Rather, there was quiet acquiescence of their common ground and a simple affirmation of the truth in her understanding of the world and the faithfulness to her own belief: *Go!* Despite differences of culture and faith, Divine Wisdom now asked her to bring her journey to fullness—to return to her home having been heard and blessed, with ears opened to all the varieties of Wisdom's voice, and heart attuned to energies that surpassed the false boundaries created by human beings. She received a mandate that carried with it the power to heal: *Go!* She went and, at the end of her journey, discovered the power of Wisdom to bless all of the generations who had come to birth and were yet to be born.

FOR REFLECTION

In what ways is the journey of my life an expression of prayer? How do I welcome reflective silence into my prayer as preparation for hearing the voice of Divine Wisdom?

How will I learn to recognize and honor the universality of Divine Wisdom wherever and however it is revealed in Creation? What is my response when I encounter an expression of Wisdom that seems foreign or difficult to comprehend?

In order to participate in breaking down the barriers that divide human beings from one another and from the rest of Creation, to which of Wisdom's many voices do I need to be more attentive? What degree of personal energy do I need to expend in identifying the common ground between these various voices?

On what levels are my intellect and heart invited to engage in a dialogue with Wisdom? As I search for Truth and Wholeness, what is Wisdom's message for me?

What word do I need to hear that will assure me of healing in my life, in the world, in Creation? This word carries with it a personal mandate; how do I envision it bringing my journey to fullness?

Openness to Receive

THE MOTHERS OF CAPERNAUM

Then they came to Capernaum; and when he was in the house he asked them, "What were you arguing about on the way?"

But they were silent, for on the way they had argued with one another who was the greatest.

He sat down, called the twelve, and said to them, "Whoever wants to be first must be last of all and servant of all."

Then he took a little child and put it among them; and taking it in his arms, he said to them, "Whoever welcomes one such child in my name welcomes me, and whoever welcomes me welcomes not me but the one who sent me."

Mark 9:33-37

The journey this time was strenuous and long, encompassing a far-ranging territory that included Tyre, Sidon, the Decapolis, Dalmanutha, Bethsaida, Caesaria Philippi, Mount Hermon, and, at last, Galilee—where he made a home in Capernaum. His energies were spent, but the knowledge that refreshment and comfort lay ahead kept his feet moving. He was only dimly aware of the heated conversation of the disciples who trailed after him, focusing instead on what lay ahead.

As he approached, the house beckoned with its stillness and the shade of its trees. He smiled to see it. He allowed himself to feel the heaviness of his body for the first time in many days and desired nothing more than to cross his home's sheltering threshold. Yet no sooner had he done this, than he found himself engulfed by those who loved him. The children, especially, greeted him with shrieks of joy and embraces around his knees, each one vying for his attention. A stream of activity continued to swirl around him, catching him up and carrying him along in its undulating eddies and rapids. Basins of clear, cool water appeared to wash the dust from the feet of the travelers. Baskets of ripe, juicy fruits were presented to refresh empty stomachs and parched tongues. The energy of the house and its inhabitants infused him with a sense of peace.

With the rituals of homecoming administered, Jesus turned his reinvigorated attention to the argument he overheard among the twelve. He inquired as to its nature, but was met with only stony, guilty silence in response. His ears had caught just enough of the conversation's import to understand they were arguing about who was the greatest among them. He turned, motioning them to follow, and sat down in the courtyard where the youngest children were playing.

Sensing movement, the children stopped and stood attentively to see what would happen next, as did their mothers who were nearby. Seeing the disciples take their places on the ground around Jesus, the children, too, seated themselves among the group, oblivious to the frantic, admonishing gestures of their mothers. The women hesitated a moment too long as they looked to one another, contemplating whether or not to try to move the children away from what could develop into a serious exchange between Teacher and disciples.

Whoever wants to be first must be last of all and servant of all. As his words faded with the breeze, Jesus smiled at the children who surrounded him and extended his arms to a willing accomplice. The little one crawled into Jesus' lap and, before he spoke again, his gaze swept the perimeter of the courtyard, where the mothers lingered in its doorways and hovered in a nervous anticipation that rivaled the pure excitement of their offspring.

Putting his arms around the child and whispering reassurances, Jesus said to all present: *Whoever welcomes one such child in my name welcomes me, and whoever welcomes me welcomes not me but the one who sent me.* The twelve who had been summoned appeared perplexed and unsettled, unsure of Jesus' meaning with regard to the subject at hand.

But when he raised his head to take in those who stood at the edges of the gathering, he was met with knowing faces that broke into shy smiles. The women understood his meaning, their worried vigilance now subsiding. Returning to their tasks, they began to share insights among themselves amidst laughter and tears.

Before you welcome a child, you must welcome your husband into your bed and heart!

At least a husband does not stay within you for nine moons!

No, but he returns as surely as the moon does!

Each time I welcomed the child within, I surrendered the functions of my body to it. It is the small one in the womb who tells me when I am hungry or tired or sick, and when it wants to be born!

Each of us brings a child into the world only by giving ourselves over to the rhythms of something greater than us.

It may be greater, but we endure the pains of labor in order to bring forth this new life. And yet, we continue to welcome each child even with the knowledge of what lies ahead!

True; and, we take each of our children to the breast when they cry because we know the intensity of our own hunger pains.

We protect and feed them, and thereby safeguard and nurture the generations not yet born.

All of those who are least able to care for themselves are a precious treasure, even when they give you no rest!

The women understood implicitly the depths of Jesus' Wisdom concerning the Domain of God. To dwell in God's Domain necessitates receptivity and surrender. To strengthen God's Domain for the children born and not yet born demands deep energy and the awareness of urgent need. Determination, perseverance, and patience, along with Wisdom and foresight, would all assist in nurturing those least able to defend themselves.

Even as the women quietly considered their own status in life—perpetual children in many ways—they began to understand the importance of what Jesus had shared with them this day. As servants to all and the last to be considered as unique individuals in their own right, they were the most like him: they could shepherd the generations to come into the Domain of God simply by their openness to receive and through their choice to serve willingly.

They already knew the great joys to be found by taking this path in life; they held the hands of each little one as they took the first steps of their life-long journeys into the heart of God. While he held a child within his embrace, Jesus revealed to the women the value of their ministry within the Domain of God and affirmed their Wisdom. Another emerging consciousness dawned among the women—they already resided in God's Domain and had much to teach young and old alike about it.

FOR REFLECTION

By what means do I sometimes brush off my work in the world as inconsequential to the unfolding of Creation? How might I envision myself as integral to the well-being of Creation?

What crosses my mind when I am asked to characterize what I do in the course of an ordinary day? In what ways could I consider my work as a valuable service or ministry?

As I open myself to all that life has to offer, do I cringe in fear of the responsibility that is entailed? How different is my reaction if I think of being receptive to life as the 'ability to respond' to whatever comes?

How willing are my heart and mind to accept my own or another's affirmation of my personal value? If asked to describe my purpose in life, what is my answer?

What are my hopes and dreams for the generations who will come after me? In what way are my contributions, right now, critical to making these hopes and dreams become reality?

Revealed in Rape

THE WOMAN ACCUSED

Early in the morning he came again to the temple… and he sat down and began to teach them.

The scribes and the Pharisees brought a woman who had been caught in adultery; and making her stand before all of them, they said to him, "Teacher, this woman was caught in the very act of committing adultery. Now in the law Moses commanded us to stone such women. Now what do you say?"

…Jesus bent down and wrote with his finger on the ground.

When they kept on questioning him, he straightened up and said to them, "Let anyone among you who is without sin be the first to throw a stone at her."

And once again he bent down and wrote on the ground.

When they heard it, they went away, one by one, beginning with the elders; and Jesus was left alone with the woman standing before him.

Jesus straightened up and said to her, "Woman, where are they? Has no one condemned you?"

She said, "No one, sir."

And Jesus said, "Neither do I condemn you. Go your way, and from now on do not sin again."

John 8:2-11

The brutality had prompted her mind to set itself free. During those eternal, pain-filled moments she found refuge in the festival song…*Out of my distress I called on the Lord; the Lord answered me and set me in a broad place. With the Lord on my side I do not fear. What can mortals do to me? The Lord is on my side to help me; I shall look in triumph on those who hate me… they surrounded me, surrounded me on every side…I shall not die, but I shall live.* Now, as she lay abused, defiled, and mocked, her clothing torn and her body exposed, every part of her being vibrated with anger and hatred; she wished him dead, along with those who found pleasure in watching. Her triumph would be to see each man struck down. *Where in this heinous act is the fruit of thanksgiving that the scribes and Pharisees proclaimed in these past days? How is this a feast of rejoicing?* Her body began to throb with the pain of the ordeal; it was nothing like the beating of her heart in the presence of love. As the sensation overwhelmed and paralyzed her, she heard the accusation that continued their assault upon her: Adulteress.

Dragged to her feet and into the sunlight, her mind tried to grasp the full weight of her sentence. *Adulteress.* The light blinded her, while at the same time it illuminated her darkened mind. *But the law demands that both man and woman discovered in this act be stoned! Where is the right hand of the Lord, the God of justice? If I must die, then so must they!* Yet, despite her triumphal fury, she knew that in acting as one, they could both condemn her and save themselves from her fate. *No one man will identify and betray another.* Waves of nausea and panic caught her spent body. *There is no one to testify to the truth. There is no one who knows my heart.*

Her heart. It had once eagerly awaited the embrace of her beloved. It had known peace and contentment. Now a poison choked it; each forced step hardened it to unforgiving stone. *Surely the Lord does not, will not forgive this vengeance exacted upon me!* Again, the words of the festival song justified her rage: *It is better to take refuge in the Lord than to put confidence in mortals…Open to me the gates of the righteous that I may enter through them.*

The sight of an accused woman incited the people they passed. Her accusers shouted her crime to the heavens as if it were not their own. Stones were gathered in hands young and old, as an impromptu procession formed in the road to the Temple. *How unlike the processions of this festival with hands holding baskets of fruit and grain!* Vile, unknowing words were shouted. *How different from the festival psalm declaring that God's steadfast love endures forever!* As her mind reeled in darkness, the mob arrived with the early light of day at the Temple. On this, the final day of the Feast of Booths, the scribes and Pharisees stopped them at the gate to the Courtyard of the Women, where a crowd was already gathered to listen to the Teacher who some called "Prophet" and others "Messiah". She heard them question her accusers as to the nature of the crime, and then felt the rough touch of these men who wore elegant garments. Suddenly, as if she herself were a small stone dropped into a silent pool of water, the crowds parted around her and formed circle within circle of gesturing hands and poised stones. She was aware of the women among them. They stood around her in solidarity and fear, their expressions telling of compassion for her plight and of deep-seated terror at what would befall them if they laid down their stones and walked away.

The only one to share the open space with her was the Teacher. His silence took in the crowd and their accusing stones. His eyes came to rest on her as she slumped to the courtyard floor, faint from thirst and exhaustion. As if in a dream, she saw him writing on the pavement with his finger. She could not decipher the exchange of words that followed, but she saw him write again before she succumbed to the blackness enveloping her. Gradually, the suffocating stillness of the crowded courtyard gave way to a gentle, refreshing breeze as person after person laid down the stones they had carried and walked away. It was this gentle caress of air that roused her to consciousness once more and lifted her to stand before the Teacher.

Woman, where are they? Has no one condemned you? As she turned to take in the scene around her—an empty courtyard with a circle of stones laying on its pavement—she realized with amazement that she was alone with the Teacher, whose eyes met hers as she sought explanation. His silence responded—a knowing silence that pierced her heart. In that moment, she knew her own murderous, triumphal rage was no different from that of the crowd's. *He knows the truth of who I am. I am indeed innocent of adultery, but my sin eats away at my heart.* His look was gentle and forgiving. Quietly she acknowledged that no one remained to accuse her, and so admitted what she had come to understand about her heart and her own great need for the compassion and forgiveness of God. *Neither do I condemn you. Go your way, and from now on do not sin again.* Humbled by what had been revealed of her body and soul, she walked slowly out of the Courtyard into a new awareness of her true self—to live.

FOR REFLECTION

As I consider the times when I have felt overwhelmed or paralyzed by the events occurring in my life, how did my body respond? What Wisdom did my body communicate to me?

When have I ever, under any circumstances, succumbed to darkness and retreated from the world surrounding me? Who or what empowered me to emerge from darkness and engage in the world again?

As I stand looking into the eyes of the woman accused, how do I perceive myself as complicit with her attackers when I face the injustice and persecution of the world with my silence and inaction? What is revealed to me in this brief encounter with the woman accused?

How do I fail to love? What do I need in order to understand my great need for compassion and forgiveness?

Do I allow myself the vulnerability of standing in a silent, open space with Jesus? Why or why not? As I consider my life, what might I expect to hear if I stood before him?

Letting Go

THE WIDOW WHO GAVE EVERYTHING

He sat down opposite the treasury, and watched the crowd putting money into the treasury…

A poor widow came and put in two small copper coins…

Then he called his disciples and said to them, "Truly I tell you, this poor widow has put in more than all those who are contributing to the treasury. For all of them have contributed out of their abundance; but she out of her poverty has put in everything she had, all she had to live on."

Mark 12:41-44

Sitting in the hollow of her hand, she thought of how meager and insufficient they would appear to those who did not know their real significance. At one time, these two copper disks were only a tiny portion of a modest inheritance she neither sought nor desired. Receiving them had meant the loss of something far greater—the source of her heart's joy. Now, these solitary remnants, these last tangible fragments of a life she still longed for, were the cause for reluctance as she thought of surrendering them to her promise.

Her promise. It had been made out of deep love and honor for the one who had gentled her heart, the one who had cared for her needs, and the one who, in the end, was unable to fulfill his obligation of simply growing old with her. She had been just a girl when they married and he a young man full of faith and ambition. Even now, she could recall their first, tentative embraces. Yet, their shy love had grown into a strong bond forged in the crucible of ordinary circumstances. It was a bond unbroken by death, invisible to the others around her who saw only her widow's garments and who felt the threat of her imminent dependence. Over these long, solitary years, she chose to live a simple life in the home they had made their own, foregoing all but what was required to sustain herself. In the face of hardship, she managed well what was left to her.

It was her choice, and hers alone, to fulfill her husband's obligation to the Temple. The Temple tax, collected after the fruits and grains of the harvest were gathered, was expected of all men who had attained the age of nineteen years. She recalled that he had shouldered it with a grateful heart. Long ago, as she sat mourning the loss of her beloved, she had determined this payment would remain a grateful expression of love—both for her husband and for God. She, too, had harvested blessings beyond measure and felt urged from deep within to give thanks and praise for the gifts of God. And so, in carefully measured portions, she made her yearly offering.

Yet, today, she was also painfully aware that, after this day's offering, only her life would remain to give in pledge—a life she dared not think of as she prepared to walk to the Temple. In this moment, full of memories and love, she cradled these two small coins as if they were the children she had been denied. She fingered their crudely struck surfaces with the gentleness of a mother wiping away a child's tear, and considered the rough stampings of an eight-rayed star on one side of each coin and an anchor on the reverse. *Will there be light in the days ahead? What will anchor me in the uncertain life I face?* No one, this day, could possibly know the emotions vying for a place within her heart. No one would guess the sadness or gratitude or fear.

With this awareness weighing heavily upon her, she stood and stepped into the sunlight. After what seemed to be an eternity of steps, she entered the colonnade surrounding the Court of the Gentiles, fully aware that only a few more steps separated her from the moment of letting go of life as she had known it. Now, clutching her precious coins, she readied her heart to journey into the unknown. Moving slowly up the five stairs leading to the east gate of the sacred enclosure, the intricate and ornate details of this beautiful gateway went unnoticed by her, so focused was her intent. She arrived at her destination—the Court of the Women wherein she would find the Temple treasury and face her uncertain future.

Hesitating on this threshold, she experienced the sensation of being watched. *How foolish. No one sees my true gift. No one knows my gratitude or my sorrow. No one cares about a solitary woman and her small treasure.* It was then that she met his eyes. Quickly, she lowered her own to stare at the stones below her feet; yet, she felt his gaze had not faltered. Looking up again, she was enveloped in the Teacher's look of compassion and understanding. Without words, without moving from the crowd surrounding him, this man held her in an embrace of solidarity that encouraged her feet to move, her hand to release the coins, and her heart to submit to the love of the One God.

It was done. She had fulfilled her promise. She had given everything she had to live on—her security, her wealth, her dreams, her trust, her hope, her faith. Turning to leave, her eyes met his once more, and she felt filled with an assurance that all would be well. With that, she moved into her new existence.

FOR REFLECTION

What is the source of my heart's joy? How do I share that joy? How do I protect it for myself?

In what ways do I attempt to live simply, choosing to focus on the gift of "blessings beyond measure"? Within the climate of contemporary culture, what mitigates against my choice for such a lifestyle?

How do I respond when I am asked to let go of someone or something precious to me? As I contemplate my response, what were the possible benefits or blessings I received as the result of a difficult letting-go experience in the past?

How can I better ready my heart each day for the journey into an unknown future? Will this be a solitary journey or is there someone who will accompany me on this journey?

As I survey my life, do I possess all that I need? What constitutes "everything I have to live on?"

Sisterhood

THE WOMEN OF MEANS AND RESOURCES

Soon afterwards he went on through cities and villages, proclaiming and bringing the good news of the kingdom of God.

The twelve were with him, as well as some women who had been cured of evil spirits and infirmities: Mary, called Magdalene, from whom seven demons had gone out, and Joanna, the wife of Herod's steward Chuza, and Susanna, and many others, who provided for them out of their resources.

Luke 8:1-3

People stared at them askance, suspicious of the women who boldly followed this Teacher from city to city in the company of men. A woman's place was in the home, not wandering about the countryside or sitting at the Teacher's feet as a disciple. Yet, in spite of the wariness that greeted them in village after village, this assembly of women possessed among themselves an obvious happiness—an infectious, alluring joy that provoked yet another kind of curiosity among the onlookers. If you were to look closely, you would see that there was not one woman like another. Individually, they exhibited various combinations of intelligence and common sense, resourcefulness and creativity, care and generosity. As a collection of individuals, they were fiercely independent—anomalies in the public world—possessed by a freedom of which most could only dream.

As women, their hearts resonated with the ancient Wisdom of the Teacher's words, as it echoed the words of their mothers and their mothers' mothers. They recognized the spirit of Yahweh's *Hokmah* in the Teacher's parables about searching and compassion. Woman by woman, they had felt the overwhelming abundance of the Teacher's compassion as it flowed through them in personal moments of healing. Each woman who made the decision to follow had known some form of brokenness in her life. Whether crippled by illness or physical infirmity, disturbed in mind or spirit, each was made whole—restored to dignity and affirmed as valuable—by the presence or touch of the Teacher. His unseen power healed the wounds each woman carried and compelled her to share this knowledge and experience of the Teacher's healing energy with others. They now lived full of gratitude, and the means for expressing this was practical.

Their very presence among the disciples who followed the Galilean Teacher incited women and men alike to attentiveness. Like bees lured by sweet flowers, the people came to gawk and investigate the purpose for such a wild assortment of followers. The presence of the women disciples provoked an openness born of natural curiosity, which in turn allowed those with ears to hear the message of the Teacher and those with eyes to see the marvels of his healing presence.

These women offered the resources at their disposal, whether trade goods or inheritance, the hospitality of their homes or the services of their households, their Wisdom or insight. They placed everything at the feet of the Teacher to further the intention of bringing forth the Divine Domain of which he spoke and announcing the invitation for all to enter.

There were hardships to endure on their journeys. Some left husbands and families behind, if they had any, while others carried babies on their hips and shepherded small children around their knees. At home, business affairs were left unattended— entrusted with hope to the hands of capable stewards. Accommodations on the road were haphazard and sometimes rough. They concealed the purses they carried, which were the targets of thievery. Many were unaccustomed to the physical strain of walking the great distances between cities and villages. Even the familiarity of their own ovens and stores of food was lost to them on the roads and hillsides. Not least, those of a certain age were governed by the courses of the moon, which either prevented them from following for a period of time or caused an embarrassing disturbance by an unexpected onset. Yet, they accompanied the Teacher undaunted, carried forward by gratitude for being returned to renewed life in the community and deep joy that they were so deeply loved by him.

Over the months, there developed among them a bond of shared purpose and mission. As the women following the Teacher joined the women of the cities or villages at synagogue, their rapt attention to the words of the Scriptures modeled the attentive openness required for discipleship. When the crowds gathered, some staying with the Teacher for days, the women disciples worked side-by-side with the women of the villages as they washed garments, drew water, or cooked meals. *Why do you follow? What is the Wisdom of the Teacher? Who is this Abba of whom he speaks and where is this "Divine Domain"? Is he the Expected One? Questions were answered, each in turn drawing listeners who eavesdropped on whispered conversations. I was given a great gift and so I follow in order that my children will know this treasure, as well. The Teacher's Wisdom is older than the knowledge of humankind; it is the Wisdom of our kinswomen who have gone before us. His Domain is not of this troubled world—there is hope for the generations to come! My heart tells me that he may, indeed, be the Messiah!* Heart spoke to heart and responses elicited further, sincere questions, allowing conversations to span the hours as tasks were completed.

Each woman spoke of her experience alone, yet together they stood on the common ground of knowing first-hand the power that emanated from the Teacher. Gradually, they wove the threads of their individual healings, their intuitive perceptions, and their unique responses to great love into a beautiful, comforting cloth of sisterhood and discipleship that invited all who touched it to share in its warmth. What began with independent, generous spirits was now a supportive and mutual solidarity of sisters who envisioned a world of love and hope for all children to come.

FOR REFLECTION

Do I believe I am truly free to choose what is life-giving? What encourages or hinders my freedom? Is there something I need to change in my life in order to exercise this freedom?

Am I capable of boldness, of going against the grain of social convention, in order to be faithful to the truth of who I am and what I have to offer to others? How have I exhibited this in the past? How can I make this a part of my future?

It is said that we teach by the example of our lives. What are the lessons to be drawn from my life? Who will benefit from this legacy of experience and knowledge?

What hardships and brokenness have I endured on my journey? What joys have resulted from these deprivations and wounds?

Who are the people I have chosen to weave into the fabric of my life in a meaningful way? What does their presence in my life teach me about human relationship and interdependence?

Dishes and Questions

MARY AND MARTHA OF BETHANY

Now as they went on their way, Jesus entered a certain village, where a woman named Martha welcomed him into her home.

She had a sister named Mary, who sat at the Lord's feet and listened to what he was saying.

But Martha was distracted by her many tasks; so she came to him and asked, "Lord, do you not care that my sister has left me to do all the work by myself? Tell her then to help me."

But the Lord answered her, "Martha, Martha, you are worried and distracted by many things; there is need of only one thing. Mary has chosen the better part, which will not be taken away from her."

Luke 10:38-42

As was his custom, Jesus sent word some days ahead of his arrival in Bethany. As head of the household, Martha received this message with great joy and gratitude, as it had been some time since she last welcomed him to her home. It would also be a relief and a blessing to greet her sister, Mary, who now traveled as one of the Teacher's followers, sitting at his feet and listening to the Wisdom he shared. Some time had passed since her sister first announced her intention to follow Jesus as a disciple. Though she had come to terms with her sister's wild notion, the itinerant lifestyle it required gave Martha no peace.

It was known that Jesus and his followers were traveling to Judea from the Galilee by way of Samaria, and this caused her no small concern for her sister's welfare. *I know that there are other women in his company, yet my sister is without kinswomen on these journeys. Should she fall ill, who is there to tend her? Does she care nothing for the risks of travel in a strange land or for her own reputation of virtue and goodness? God alone knows how I tried to talk sense into her! Yet, did she listen to me as she does to him? No! Of course not!* Emotions tumbled in and out of Martha's heart and mind, rapidly exchanging relief for worry, worry for frustration, and frustration for resignation. Still, she began her preparations and as she worked, her heart grew lighter in anticipation of their arrival.

With the break of day, golden light spilled down the eastern face of the Mount of Olives like oil poured slowly from a jar. Standing at the courtyard door, she looked down the slope toward the road leading into Bethany, where the contrast between light and shadow resembled her own ambivalence about what the day would bring. *Surely, my sister will remain this time. She will bake with me and help me to prepare the dishes required by so many people. We will talk and remember our time as young girls… But, how can I be sure of this? She has traveled far and perhaps our bond is strained by the distance. I wish I knew.* The aroma of fresh bread reached her and drew her back to her work.

When she returned to the threshold of her home, there below, still some distance away, were the travelers she expected. As they climbed upward, she recognized Jesus at first glance. *He has not changed much. Good food and rest will refresh his countenance.* Her eyes continued to search for her only sister. Finally, their eyes met and smiles of greeting were exchanged. *She is glad to be home. Perhaps nothing has really changed between us.* She turned away to ready the water and cloths that would wash away the dust and heat of travel.

Returning once again to the doorway, Martha welcomed all with the hospitality of her home and the excitement of her heart. She moved from one task to another seamlessly, the result of many years of managing a household. Bread, olive oil, dates, figs, and nuts appeared for refreshment as stories of their travels began to emerge. Moving about briskly, she caught only bits and pieces of what was said, while at the same time she noticed her sister remained still and attentive to the words of Jesus. *Is she so weary from her travel that she is not able to attend to the household responsibilities as she once did? Does she not care that I need her hands as well to make everyone comfortable? Mary smiles, but why will she not speak to me and ask how she may be of assistance? Stubborn, arrogant girl!*

Unanswered questions led to anger. She grumbled under her breath about the requests and demands of the guests. She grabbed baskets and poured wine carelessly. *How dare she ignore me and the hospitality of this home—her home! Why, I have a mind to…* Her thought was interrupted as she noticed Jesus standing apart from the others, but it resumed its fury as she approached him with a blaming tone of voice… *Do you not care that my sister has left me to do all the work by myself? Tell her then to help me.* Surprised and somewhat amused by this woman who was like a sister to him, Jesus looked at her for a few moments with wide eyes. *Martha, Martha.* Shaking his head, he chided her gently, the same way her brother Lazarus still did and had since the time they were children together. Disarmed by the sound of Jesus' voice, she knew he would not be fooled by her anger. He knew her well enough to understand the worry she had for her sister and the weight of the household that had come to rest on her shoulders. He knew her as a woman filled with the Wisdom of service and hospitality, nourishment and beauty, practicality and good judgment—the epitome of the valiant woman of the book of Proverbs.

Squaring her shoulders, Martha acknowledged her distraction and worry about many things, just as he had said. Yet she resisted his implication that every person must choose only the one thing in life resonant with the truth of the gifts and talents given to them by God. *Hah! Wouldn't I be grateful for a life without dishes?* He continued to look at her, this time with a quizzical expression that tested the truth of her heart. *He acknowledges my fears for my sister's safety in the public realm. He knows I prefer that my sister be less brash and simply come home to attend to the chores of the household. Yet, why must he defend her by saying, "Mary has chosen the better part and it will not be taken from her"?*

Then, it struck her. *The better part.* In very few words, Jesus had blessed not only her sister's life, but her own as well. Their individual needs, their abilities, their choices blended into the dance of God's work in the world. The energy of God coursed through both her cooking and her sister's attentive listening, igniting each of their spirits as disciples of Wisdom.

FOR REFLECTION

Is it self-limiting to not realize or admit to the fullness of my gifts and talents? As I name the extent of these in my life, what might I be called upon to do because of them?

When frustration and anger build within me, have I ever allowed these emotions to blind me to the possibilities that exist for becoming who God desires me to be? How might I choose to diffuse these emotions in order to see my options more clearly?

Do I harbor jealousy toward those who have discovered their "better part" in life? What would release me from this state of mind and heart?

How difficult is it for me to allow myself the flexibility and openness of a both/and perspective, rather than to view my life as a series of either/or choices? What would the ramifications of such a perspective be on my life?

What is the unique, sacred power of my life? How does this power inspire wonder and awe in me? What generates fear in me—possible inadequacy, mediocrity, greatness?

Blessed

THE WOMAN
WHO HEARD THE WORD OF GOD

A woman in the crowd raised her voice
and said to Jesus,
"Blessed is the womb that bore you
and the breasts that nursed you!"

But he said,
"Blessed rather are those
who hear the word of God and obey it!"

Luke 11:27-28

She was a woman wise of age and experience who had nothing to lose and possibly something to gain. For days upon days, drawn on by an irresistible urge to hear and see more, she pursued the Teacher in spiraling patterns around the Mount of Olives, trudging from the gardens of Gethsemane, past numerous olive presses and around to Bethany—along with the multitude of others who formed a somewhat ragtag assembly. *Let us see if there is something in his words that will point to some new insight, something that has escaped my attention. He is obviously Wisdom's child. The words that flow from his mouth captivate me. My imagination soars, my heart leaps, and my mind longs to explore!* Maturity indeed allowed a bit of boldness to emerge in her thoughts—a silent challenge both to herself and the Teacher to stretch past the limits of what was commonly known and understood. Her spirit hungered and longed to be filled to overflowing by this child of Holy Wisdom.

Wisdom did not reside solely in the Teacher's words, however. Only moments before, she had watched as he drew voice out of one who was mute and bestowed the blessing of words! Awestruck, she felt something stir inside her breast as she attempted to clear her mind and make sense of what had just transpired. Unbidden, familiar words emerged from the Scriptures: *For wisdom is more mobile than any motion; because of her pureness she pervades and penetrates all things, for she is a breath of the power of God…she can do all things, and while remaining in herself, she renews all things…In every generation she passes into holy souls and makes them friends of God, and prophets.* Somewhere deep within, she grasped a tiny fragment of truth and held on to it tenaciously, afraid it might slip away as suddenly as it had appeared. The words of Scripture suddenly began to take on new significance. An emergent awareness surged through her and caused her to feel as if she would burst if she did not engage this figure of Wisdom in dialogue.

Aware of the fortunate circumstance before her, she raised her own voice above the murmuring crowd: *Blessed is the womb that bore you and the breasts that nursed you!* Jesus recognized her invitation to enter into the game of Wisdom, the call and response of wit and riddle, nuanced with its earthy undertones of sensuality. She was openly testing him and expected a shrewd retort, but not the one she received. Smiling broadly, he shouted back: *Blessed rather are those who hear the word of God and obey it!*

Time stood still as her awareness was pulled in several directions at once. *I hear some of those around me whispering in agreement, for surely the mother of this man should be blessed for the great work of raising so wise and compassionate a son—a son who lives daily in the heart of God's Hokmah. Yet, I intended far more than this by my words; it is only proper to acknowledge that Lady Wisdom invigorates the Teacher's words and work. In both senses, I invited him to accept the truth that the origins of his power lay outside of himself. His answer, though, veers away from the logical response of agreement that it is the son who is blessed by such a mother. What am I to make of his puzzling answer?*

The crowd seemed to increase during their brief exchange; whether it was in numbers or intensity she could not determine. She felt, however, the pressing weight and tension of both the crowd and the dialectic exchange throughout her body. Jesus went on with his teaching as she turned his response over in her mind and heart, considering what he intended it to mean. Dimly, she heard him speak of the queen of the South who journeyed far from home to listen to the Wisdom of Solomon and her attention was aroused once again with his next words: *See, something greater than Solomon is here! No one after lighting a lamp puts it in a cellar, but on the lampstand so that those who enter may see the light.*

The meaning of his words dawned slowly inside her, raising layers of understanding as subtle, yet also as brilliant, as the emerging colors of the sun appearing over the horizon. *The Teacher countered my Wisdom utterance by pointing not to his mother or even Wisdom herself, but instead to me! He tells me to listen to the Word of God in my own experience, to the same Word that urged me to speak out in public, to the Word that convinced me of the veracity of his teaching, to the Word that requires my response! I am to obey it and trust my inner knowing; I am to allow Wisdom's light to be seen. The power of Wisdom is made visible in my words, through my acts of healing and compassion, in how I nurture those around me, and most especially with my ability to listen and discern Wisdom's desires in my heart.*

The sun continued its course through the sky that day, and she turned her thoughts around and around as if examining jewels in the light. With the setting of the sun, there came a gentle realization: *I am surprised by and grateful for the blessing of this day!*

FOR REFLECTION

When have I evidenced the attitude that there is nothing more to learn? Under what circumstances has the sometimes difficult process of maturity pushed me to exhibit trepidation because I might be stretched far beyond my comfort level?

When was the last time I felt the deep excitement of apprehending a new awareness? As I grow older, do I remain capable of grasping a tiny fragment of truth and holding on to it tenaciously? How might the fear that truth could slip away as suddenly as it had appeared motivate my desire for it?

Am I capable of being surprised, or do I live with rigid expectations of what should happen next? What would allow me to spontaneously burst out of my mindset or limitations?

As I wrestle with ideas or truths that I encounter in my daily life, what processes do I engage to determine whether or not they apply to me? How do I carve out space in my life for quiet discernment?

Do I trust the Word of God I hear within my mind and heart, or do I assume what I hear is only my own ego playing games with me? How do I know the difference?

Earth and Light

THE WOMAN BENT DOUBLE

Now he was teaching in one of the synagogues on the sabbath.

And just then there appeared a woman with a spirit that had crippled her for eighteen years. She was bent over and was quite unable to stand up straight.

When Jesus saw her, he called her over and said, "Woman, you are set free from your ailment."

When he laid his hands on her, immediately she stood up straight and began praising God.

Luke 13:10-13

She had been ill for eighteen years. During those long years, the disease ravaged and broke her body so badly that she was bent over double, forced to contemplate the dust of the earth rather than the brilliance of the light. She could not straighten up; movement was pain-filled and awkward. As she made her way through the streets of the village toward the sanctuary of the synagogue, she was subjected to the jostling of the crowds and the crush of the marketplace. Yet, she felt within herself the strength of a desire that soared beyond her limitations and a courage that propelled the tremendous physical effort it would take to make her way to this house of prayer.

The strength of her spirit was tested daily. To present herself for prayer in the synagogue today was to continue the risk of placing herself in judgment before the community. With a heaviness of heart weighing more cruelly on her than her deformity, she knew with certainty, in her neighbors' minds, this illness that plagued her was caused by an evil spirit, most certainly the result of sin. *What do they know? They cannot see the goodness of my heart.* And so she chose to display her infirmity for all to see, knowing within that it spoke of her deep and trusting relationship with God and the great longing with which she sought God's comforting love.

Worse still, every villager seemed to be at the synagogue today. *What will they say to me? Will they shun my presence yet again?* Yet their very numbers seemed to render her small and stooped presence invisible. She moved inconspicuously through the ocean of their bodies, unseen as they strained to glimpse the itinerant Prophet visiting their humble synagogue. How she was noticed by him would remain a mystery to her for the remainder of her life. Yet, at some point in the Prophet's teaching, this Jesus noticed her and called out to her: *Woman, you are free from your sickness!*

Walking across the room, and risking his own public reputation and religious purity, he approached her boldly and touched her compassionately, placing his hands on her. At once, a multiplicity of feelings and sensations coursed through her, allowing her worn and fragile body to respond as it had not been able to for many years. With an impulse that originated in the depths of her being, she was able to straighten her bent frame, raise her eyes from the dust, and praise God. This Prophet did not lift her contorted body, but the power and energy of his compassionate love somehow healed her inability to face the world and the light. As she once again stood upright with the supple spine of a young girl, her eyes met those of the man Jesus. She knew in that instant she would never again know the absence of the Light in her life.

FOR REFLECTION

Where in my body or spirit do I carry the broken and ravaged elements of my life? In my day-to-day existence, how do I seek out healing for the damage and hurt that I carry?

In what ways do I persist in contemplating the dust of life, rather than the light? What holds me back from raising my eyes to the light?

Do I possess a heaviness of heart that prevents me from acknowledging my physical, mental, or spiritual infirmities? What would help me to choose instead to see and soar beyond the limits of these frailties?

Perhaps in spite of a great longing to be known for the truth of who I am, how do I attempt to convince myself that I am inconspicuous to others, to God, and even to myself? Why do I feel the need to hide at times and not be noticed?

How do I respond to the energy of light when I am exposed to it? What are the similarities in my response to the Light of Christ when the depths of my being are addressed by the Word?

No Longer Cast Aside

THE WOMEN OF JUDEA

Jesus left Galilee and went to the region of Judea beyond the Jordan.

Large crowds followed him, and he cured them there.

Some Pharisees came to him, and to test him they asked, "Is it lawful for a man to divorce his wife for any cause?"

He answered, "Have you not read that the one who made them at the beginning 'made them male and female', and said, 'For this reason a man shall leave his father and mother and be joined to his wife, and the two shall become one flesh'? So they are no longer two, but one flesh. Therefore what God has joined together, let no one separate."

They said to him, "Why then did Moses command us to give a certificate of dismissal and to divorce her?"

He said to them, "It was because you were so hard-hearted that Moses allowed you to divorce your wives, but at the beginning it was not so. And I say to you, whoever divorces his wife, except for unchastity, and marries another commits adultery."

Matthew 19:1-9

Word arrived early in the morning that a traveling Storyteller was approaching from the north with large crowds behind him—reliable testimony of his ability with words. Rumors also abounded about the traveler's skill with healing. It was said that many who followed him had been wondrously cured of conditions borne since they took their first breaths. Still, it was not so much the possibility of seeing such healings as it was the prospect of time away from the routine of ordinary things that prompted excitement among the women. While their husbands offered stern warnings to tend to the work of the day, these cautions were tempered by the women's knowledge that, if they worked quickly, there would be sufficient time to prepare small bundles of food to carry along to the place where the crowds would gather. Without question, the swells of people would converge near the waters of the nearby Jordan where the promise of a cool breeze and a few precious hours of recreation lingered.

Whole families emerged from their homes, each man leading his own small exodus to the river. Older children ran ahead of their mothers and grandmothers, calling to playmates. The women followed, shepherding younger children and carrying provisions for the excursion. Greetings were called out and smiles erupted into quiet laughter. Comparisons were exchanged as to the contents of their bundles and promises of shared delicacies made up for the haphazard nature of the quickly assembled meals. *Don't worry! I have figs for three families, but could you spare some bread? Who do you think might have more honey than she needs for her family? I am sure I saw someone carrying a jar of olives. A cistern of water will not be sufficient in this day's heat!* Their chatter was like that of sisters who shared the same daily expectations, demands and anxieties—and who understood the value of this journey for one another's spirits. Each of them lived in the tenuous embrace of her husband's approval; there was great risk in provoking displeasure. Generations of their kinswomen had lived with the same threat of divorce for the slightest of grievances—real or imagined. Only recently had the rabbis argued about valid provocation for a decree of divorce. Some said any reasonable displeasure on the part of a husband was cause for removing a wife; others argued only adultery was justifiable cause.

Today, near the banks of the Jordan, they dismissed thoughts of this nature to revel in the luxury of a few hours of storytelling, the sounds of the wind and river, and the dazzling array before them of people gathered from across the Decapolis. Having traveled south from the Galilee, down the eastern edge of the Jordan, this storytelling Healer drew the curiosity of people from village and city alike. The ordinary thoughts of the women swirled now with the presumed grandeur to be found in the markets and theaters of Hippos, Gadara, and Pella. For a short while, they could imagine themselves as being a part of something much larger than the immediate, domestic world they knew.

Not unlike the times when the Storyteller was said to have dramatically healed bodies trapped by disease or death, to gather for the telling of Wisdom parables in public was a time of healing liberation rarely afforded these women of Judea. *Can you smell the Jordan's waters? See the richness and beauty of the fabrics used in that garment! My body feels quiet and still.* Here beside the life-giving waters of the river and under the open expanse of sky, there was a visible release of worry and tension among them.

But the restorative quality of the day was soon interrupted by a parade of Pharisees who made their way brusquely to the Weaver of Parables, parting the crowds as they went. Their self-importance was obvious to the women who looked on with impatient disinterest. *Why must they bring their pompous questions and arguments now? Who do they think they are to disrupt the blessing of this day? There are so few hours before we must return to our homes; when will they go?* The multitude settled into relative silence to hear the exchange that had already begun, while only the children seemed able to hold on to the joy of the occasion.

A question was presented with great voice to the Storyteller—intended as challenge and spectacle at one and the same time. It caught the ears of the women present as if it were spoken directly into their hearts. *Is it lawful for a man to divorce his wife for any cause?* Confusion ensued in whispered conversations. *Are they inquiring about a husband's right to dismiss his wife for any reason, or do they hope that this man will announce only those causes he considers lawful?* With bated breath, the women strained to hear the Parable Weaver's response as they watched the faces of their husbands.

What they heard was a recounting of the story of Creation. He spoke of God's Creation, of wholeness between male and female, and of the completion of one another as participation in the work of Divine Creation. His words described the original blessing of human nature and the sacred desire and need of man and woman for one another. His retelling of the story from the Torah ended on the emphatic note that no person could destroy the oneness intended by God. Furtive glances were exchanged among the women; eyes spoke silent questions about the effect of these words. Within the space of a heartbeat, one Pharisee asked boldly why Moses conceded to divorce and the Storyteller's response was quick, certain and scathing: *It was because you were so hard-hearted.*

Shock and surprise rippled through the women listening to these words. If the Storyteller's interpretation of the Scriptures was true, then the cause for divorce was not rooted in inconsequential accusations leveled because of displeasure but in their husbands' deeper, unyielding inability to see their wives as little more than property to be disposed of at will. His words raised all women to the dignity of an inseparable element of the whole as intended by God—an identity capable of yielding a new kind of freedom and liberation. As the words sank more deeply into their consciousness, the women reawakened to an inner knowledge that had been suppressed in them by fear: Divine intention is greater than the law of man!

Except for unchastity. The women were caught short by the blunt force of the cautionary tone issued by this Weaver of Parables who knew the details of the Creation story so fully. It was well-known among all Jews that a chaste person stood before God with a heart pure and open to love, a heart that reverenced another with the gift of self. Their feminine hearts were being called to liberation through the recognition of their utter dependence on God and to an awareness of mutual responsibility with their husbands. If no longer considered the property of their husbands, the women were now called to the constant effort of creating life and love out of their mistakes and failings. No longer would they see themselves as passive partners in their relationships, but instead as the ones who contributed to the integrity and goodness of the union. Failure on the part of either man or woman to bring about wholeness in their mutual relationship would cause each to become less than what God intended.

It was not difficult for the women to each recall, in the private sanctuary of her heart, the words of the great Song of Solomon: *I am my beloved's and my beloved is mine.* It was evident from their faces and the silence that drifted over them. The words of the Storyteller resonated with a sense of inner worth in which the women knew themselves as beloved and understood themselves to be the revelation of the countenance of God for their husbands. Walking home, warm glows graced their faces and there was no evidence of self-satisfaction as the result of this deeper consciousness. They seemed to stand and move with greater dignity—and freedom of heart.

FOR REFLECTION

What realistic impact does the call to wholeness and chaste living have on my life? What are my perceptions of it as possibly restrictive or limiting? How might it be a liberating invitation for me?

Under what circumstances am I prone to assuming someone else's shortcomings or failures as my own? What pressures compel me to do this?

When do I minimize or deny my own desires and needs in favor of placing a greater priority on satisfying the demands of others? What motivates me to do this—duty, love, fear, my need to control difficult situations, or something else?

Do I believe that I am meant to reveal the face of God to others? How would this awareness enhance my ability to be deeply present to the Divine spark in others?

If I am called to be chaste in all of my relationships (with self, others, Earth, and God), how do I intend to become more fully integrated and self-aware over the course of my lifetime? How will I accomplish the paradigm shift necessary to envision all of life as an expression of the Divine?

To Drink the Cup

THE MOTHER OF JAMES AND JOHN

Then the mother of the sons of Zebedee came to him with her sons, and kneeling before Jesus, she asked a favor of him.

And he said to her, "What do you want?"

She said to him, "Declare that these two sons of mine will sit, one at your right hand and one at your left, in your kingdom."

But Jesus answered, "You do not know what you are asking. Are you able to drink the cup that I am about to drink?"

They said to him, "We are able."

Many women were also there, looking on from a distance; they had followed Jesus from Galilee and had provided for him.

Among them were Mary Magdalene, and Mary the mother of James and Joseph, and the mother of the sons of Zebedee.

Matthew 20:20-22; 27:55-56

Images from the preceding weeks filled her mind. She marveled at the healings of women and children, of the ones whose minds were without peace, of the blind and the paralyzed, of those without voice. She remembered each one in vivid detail. They formed a kind of mosaic, each piece part of a whole that was slowly forming, though she could not yet envision its completion.

It was overwhelming to look out over the mass of people who crowded around her to hear Jesus' teaching. *Where do they all come from? Why do they come? His parables speak of a kingdom, God's kingdom, a Divine Domain. Are we not already God's chosen ones? He fills them with hope of a new order, yet how and when will this Domain be established? Is this why my sons chose to leave their nets behind? Is there a place for them in this new kingdom?*

In the midst of her efforts to arrange the mosaic in her mind, she struggled greatly to make sense of what was being revealed to her. The piece that did not seem to fit in any fashion caused disruption in the depths of her heart: *Why did I follow them?*

Recalling the past, she knew she had always relied upon her woman's instinct to protect and nurture life; it served her well as her family grew. On that long ago day by the shore when she watched her adult sons walk away into an unknown future—so too did she find herself trailing protectively behind. Her instincts as a mother had urged her on that day to shield them, yet even now she chided herself for her efforts. *What did I think I could do for them, grown men that they are? They have no children of their own, but they walked away from their father and their work to wander around, following this Teacher, Jesus. So, here I am watching and listening to discover my own purpose. May Wisdom enlighten me! Do not reveal me as unwise!*

As their company continued this journey to Jerusalem, her mother's heart was touched by the gentleness of Jesus as he gathered children to his side and blessed them. He seemed to look into their small faces with the eyes of a mother, revealing great love and patience for their antics. Moving farther on, he stopped to tell the story of the owner of a vineyard who hired laborers to tend his crop. At the end of the day's labor, the landowner chose to give equal wages to all he employed and, when challenged, he defended his action by declaring he could be generous with what belonged to him with whomever he chose. *He knows the generous love of a mother; he reveals his own generosity in the telling of this tale. Here is the task I am called to—I must intercede and prevail on his generosity to quell my concern for the welfare of my children. My sons need a place in this kingdom of his.*

In a quiet moment, when the people had dispersed to their homes for the evening and only the disciples remained, she approached Jesus and knelt before him in an attitude of supplication. Turning to her, he inquired as to her need, whereupon she traced out the plan she had in mind for her sons: places of honor in this new Domain. She did not dare to look up. After what seemed an eternity, his response shocked her with its invective tone: *You do not know what you are asking. Are you able to drink the cup that I am about to drink?* Without conscious awareness, she responded, along with her sons, *We are able.*

Having declared herself able, her mind instantly collided against the words from the book of Lamentations. *Rejoice and be glad, O daughter Edom, you that live in the land of Uz; but to you also the cup shall pass; you shall become drunk and strip yourself bare.* Alarmed and unsettled, she scarcely heard anything that transpired from that moment forward. The words turned over in her mind again and again, interlaced with insights and questions. *Edom was a rich seat of Wisdom. Yes, there is joy and gladness in the company of Holy Wisdom. But, what is this cup I have sworn to drink from? The cup of God is not painless to consume, as witnessed by our ancestors. Why am I accused with these words of complicity with drunken nakedness? What is the meaning of this? Why did I follow them into such an answer?*

With every step of the slow journey south, through all the succeeding months, the questions followed her. Among the Teacher's followers, no one suspected what challenges lay ahead of their entry into the holy city of Jerusalem, where a tumultuous greeting awaited. The ensuing days overflowed with contradiction. Lessons and parables that spoke of justice and great love clashed with actions of anger and obliteration. Moments of healing compassion contrasted boldly with heated accusations. Promise existed beside desolation. In the end, all of her inner strength was necessary to watch the ebbing of life and energy in the last days of Jesus. *This is the burden a mother accepts without hesitation. This is the cup of which he spoke. I am called to give testimony to his life with my presence. No child of Wisdom should endure the unthinkable without the energy of love to stand guard in defiance of destruction.*

And thus, she found herself following a son again, this time with the grace of Holy Wisdom guiding her steps. She walked with him to share her spirit as he struggled; she stood erect in defiance of hatred and jealousy to give him strength. As she willed herself to confront death and not to look away, her thoughts drifted to the sons she had birthed. *They are not here. They are not here.* Conscious of their absence, the Scriptures came to her once more: *They mounted up to heaven, they went down to the depths; their courage melted away in their calamity; they reeled and staggered like drunkards, and were at their wits end.*

It was immediately apparent to her that a human being can become drunk on many things in life. One can fill a cup with suffering and be overcome by fear, confusion, and anguish. On the other hand, the cup of suffering brings into existence wisdom, courage, and love. Both cups hold the power to strip one bare; both reveal so much to the world. She knew herself to be a daughter of Wisdom, a disciple of the Christ. To drink of the cup meant that she could no longer merely follow. She saw that every step of her journey had exposed a precious glimpse of herself, each a tessera that formed the mosaic of her life. Now complete, the mosaic revealed the portrait of a courageous woman who would lead other daughters and sons to truth and Wisdom—to the Christ, the revelation of Wisdom.

FOR REFLECTION

As I look back over my life, when and under what circumstances did my journey show me to be a follower? Why did I choose to follow at those times?

In my concern for the welfare of others, when have I paused to examine my motives and actions? Upon introspection, did I act selflessly in those instances or were there other agendas behind my behaviors?

Thinking of a time when I have been called upon to lead, what was my first reaction to the invitation? Why did I either embrace the occasion as an opportunity for growth, or refuse and shrink back out of fear?

What constitutes a leader? What natural strengths of character and spirit allow me to contemplate the personal possibility of leadership?

In which of my life roles do I know myself as a true leader? Who looks to my experience and wisdom for guidance?

Grief Expressed

THE SISTERS OF LAZARUS

When Jesus arrived, he found that Lazarus had already been in the tomb four days.

When Martha heard that Jesus was coming, she went and met him, while Mary stayed at home.

Martha said to Jesus, "Lord, if you had been here, my brother would not have died."

She went back and called her sister Mary, and told her privately, "The Teacher is here and is calling for you."

And when she heard it, she got up quickly and went to him.

When Mary came where Jesus was and saw him, she knelt at his feet and said to him, "Lord, if you had been here, my brother would not have died."

When Jesus saw her weeping…he was greatly disturbed in spirit and deeply moved.

Jesus began to weep.

John 11:17, 20-21, 28-29, 32-33, 35

They approached life from different directions, owing to the diversity of gifts bestowed upon them by God. Without always agreeing, the sisters respected the few freedoms of choice they each possessed and guarded them with the defensive, protective ferocity of lionesses against the encroachment of their society's patriarchal limitations. Yet, as sisters they held between them a common thread of love that tied their hearts together and bound them with a silent language. Born into the proximity of blood relationship, they had grown to know the implied meanings and nuances of one another's tone of voice, as well as the unspoken words of their bodies. Nevertheless, it was the invisible filament between the two hearts of these women that resonated with the vibration of each other's energy and elicited an empathetic response before words of any sort could be spoken.

In the desperation that washed over them with the deteriorating health of their brother Lazarus, the sisters gave mutual, tacit permission for emotions to overtake them without judgment. At times they wept in one another's arms, while at other moments they sought the refuge of solitude or activity to assuage the pain and fill the anticipatory emptiness of loss. Each sister knew implicitly what was required by her kinswoman through the long, slow process of letting go, protected her right to express herself as needed, and provided the space for the course of its movement to take place, despite the arrival of mourners.

Knowing death to be imminent, the mourners arrived like harbinger flocks of ravens or vultures, circling and lingering until death presented itself. In this disconcerting atmosphere, the women received word that Jesus, who was as much a brother to them as Lazarus, was nearby in Jerusalem. They sent a message to him in haste. *Lord, he whom you love is ill.* Lazarus died, however, almost as soon as word was sent. Four days, however, would elapse before Jesus arrived in Bethany, and the delay provoked unanswerable questions between the sisters. *Why does he not come? Where is the urgency of love he has professed to us? We have welcomed him into our home as we would family and instead we receive this spiteful disregard in thanks? What provokes him to do such a thing?* Disappointment and disbelief gave way to outrage and accusation, vented in both thought and impatience. Those who had traveled from Jerusalem to comfort the sisters now seemed more like pelicans that had gorged themselves on the emotion and hospitality of the sisters' home and were unable to move. *Where is he whom we need?*

Where, indeed, was he? Taken up by a mission he did not quite understand fully and filled with the same childish pride he had acted upon at the age of twelve, Jesus chose to remain in Jerusalem, ignoring the pull of his own heart. Despite deep love for these three who were like his own human family, he settled on purposeful delay as a means of showing God's care and compassion. *Our friend Lazarus has fallen asleep, but I am going there to awaken him. For your sake I am glad I was not there, so that you may believe.* Somewhere in his deep center, he recognized his own human arrogance—all too late.

In characteristic fashion, each sister responded in her own manner to his eventual arrival: one bursting forth with intercepting confrontation, the other choosing measured receptiveness. The common ground between these varied reactions, though, owed its existence to the resonant chord linking their hearts as one. The first words out of each woman's mouth were identical: *Lord, if you had been here, my brother would not have died.* The words accused him, implored justification for such harshness, despaired of his apathy, and questioned the veracity of his heart.

His reassurances to the sisters at first seemed feeble and incomprehensible in the face of their pain. But the power of their common grief opened a channel that permitted the deepest energies of their hearts to vibrate with significant and perceptive love. Lured by something beyond the immediacy of death, one sister acceded to the remnant hope of deliverance by the Messiah and professed affirmation in answer to his heart's question: *Do you believe this?* The other heard his longing and knelt at Jesus' feet to reverence this energy of the heart. She was suffused with the sense of his desperate need to lament, to be healed of the wounds caused by his refusal to respond out of pure compassion, and this allowed her to weep openly as she led him to the tomb. Countenancing the overwhelming expression of grief by all who followed them to the tomb caused a breach in the wall around Jesus' emotions. As he looked at the tear-streaked faces of these women whom he loved, the barrier he had erected within himself fell completely, and he began to weep. He realized that he had abandoned them in the immediacy of their need and subsequent grief. He had neglected the brotherhood he knew with Lazarus. He had forgotten, because of the strength of his own interior struggles, that his Abba's Domain resided deep within every element of Creation and was strengthened through even the smallest of compassionate actions.

The sisters watched as this realization overwhelmed Jesus. Somehow, through their power to express and understand the faults and deep desires of their hearts, Jesus' own heart had been freed.

FOR REFLECTION

How often am I capable of expressing my emotions without self-judgment or self-criticism? What circumstances prompt me to protect and defend my own emotional needs or those of others?

If I know what it is to abandon, or be abandoned by, love, how deep were the effects of the experience on me? What elements of my person were stymied? Which dimensions were freed as a result?

What is there an urgency to love in my life? How does it manifest itself? What might provoke me to ignore it?

How different would my life choices be if my heart and emotions were consistently involved in determining the criteria for action? What happens when I rely solely on my intellect to make decisions?

What prompts the deepest core of my being to weep when I look at myself, others or the world? How is my empathetic response to the needs of the world essential to realizing the Domain of God?

Remembered

THE WOMAN WITH AN ALABASTER JAR

While Jesus was at Bethany in the house of Simon the leper, as he sat at the table, a woman came with an alabaster jar of very costly ointment of nard, and she broke open the jar and poured the ointment on his head.

But some were there who said to one another in anger, "Why was the ointment wasted in this way? For this ointment could have been sold for more than three hundred denarii, and the money given to the poor."

And they scolded her.

But Jesus said, "Let her alone; why do you trouble her? She has performed a good service for me. For you always have the poor with you, and you can show kindness to them whenever you wish; but you will not always have me. She has done what she could; she has anointed my body beforehand for its burial. Truly I tell you, wherever the good news is proclaimed in the whole world, what she has done will be told in remembrance of her."

Mark 14:3-9

The alabastron was luminous in her hand. The curved, sinuous surface of the stone absorbed the sunlight that moved through it. The stone appeared to glow as if the light emanated from within. Simultaneously, where the sun's rays glinted off the polished shell of the vessel, it scattered bits of reflected light onto her hand. She delighted in holding this small container with its sweet promise of the future. Rocking the ointment pot to and fro in a bright shaft of light, she watched the viscous nard it held flow slowly in unison with the movement of her hand. *The distance this oil travels now is so short compared to the great distance it traveled from its source in faraway mountains, over caravan roads, and through foreign lands.* She could only imagine the true value of this gift she had received from her mother and father. *Someday, I will offer it to my husband lavishly. I will pour it out with abandon as I give myself to him and prostrate myself at his feet—both of us ready to pour forth our lives into one another.*

With tender contemplation, her finger traced the subtle, spiraling bands of colored stone that grew smaller as they approached the neck of the bottle. She caressed the tiny, delicately carved and pierced ears of the flask that held a thin cord. Thus absorbed, her thoughts drifted to the hope that one day she, in the manner of the matriarch Ruth, would recognize the one for whom the oil was intended, a man of compassion and integrity. *It was through Ruth that life and leadership were restored to Israel; I, too, want to discover the promise of new life and give everything to show the way for our people. Solomon's Song tells of a king anointed with fragrant oil. Do I dare hope for such a love, upon whose head I will pour the contents of this vial? Will my story be worthy of telling by the generations to come?*

There was no time for daydreaming, though, in the days leading to the Passover festival. She was roused by the tongues of the other women who urged her to busy herself with the tasks at hand. Reluctantly, she placed the vessel's graceful thread around her neck. The provisions particular to this feast would be assembled and their homes would be purged of all leavening. Herbs would be collected. Wood and kindling would be gathered in order to roast the lambs for each family. Yet, as she and the other women went about their work, they were keenly aware of the tension that flowed down into Bethany from the land beyond the Mount of Olives, from beyond the Kidron Valley, even from Jerusalem itself.

Pilgrims were coming to the holy city for the festival in great numbers. They swelled the population and strained the accommodations and resources of the place. The Temple precincts were inundated with men, women, and children, exchanging money and purchasing the unblemished lambs required for the Passover meal. The market stalls did brisk business supplying the goods travelers had been unable to bring with them. Among the throngs, Jesus and his followers had arrived some days before, staying in Bethany with friends in the evenings and spending the hours of daylight in Jerusalem. Despite his angry outburst among the merchants in the porticoes surrounding the Temple, the crowds continued to gather around him in the courtyards as he taught, and his stories and teachings made their way back to Bethany each night, retold for the benefit and enjoyment of all. He had also spoken, however, in cautionary tones of things to come—of destruction, war, and persecution—and there was much confusion and fear among his listeners. His authority to teach had been called into question by the chief priests; he accused the Sadducees of Scriptural ignorance; and, he denounced the vanity and hypocrisy of the scribes openly. It was well-known that many considered him a threat. Even here, in the relative safety of Bethany, his followers were anxious for his well-being and questioned his brash behavior.

She clung to the shadows each evening, watching him ascend the hill on which Bethany sat as he returned from Jerusalem with the disciples. Tonight, he looked worn and tired—not at all like a man who had counseled the crowd only hours beforehand to keep alert, to be on watch, and to stay awake. *No, he is no longer alert; rather, he is spent. But see, he carries himself with the dignity of a loyal and loving servant who persists out of duty. His shoulders tell of how he has shared his energy with those who came to him in need. He has poured forth his healing and compassion, emptying himself. What does he need? Refreshment and sleep, of course. How I wish there was something I could do.*

Unbidden, a deep desire to serve and comfort him made its presence known. It led her to the house of Simon, where Jesus was invited to dine as a gesture of gratitude for healing his host of an alienating condition. *I am not an invited guest. What am I doing here? I have nothing, nothing to offer him. And, why do I feel I must respond to his needs through my desire to attend him? What will it matter to him if I do or don't do something? He does not call for me.* Yet she could not will her feet to return home. Instead, there was an incessant tugging at her heart that pulled her forward into the room where the guests were beginning to recline at table. Wanting to protect herself from the pulling force, her hand went to her breast and met with the alabastron that hung from her neck. Shocked by its presence, she looked at it for a few moments, considering its intended purpose. *It is to be given to a man who moves my heart and to whom I can give what is mine to give—comfort and compassion, reverence and fidelity.*

She moved to Jesus' place at the table with purpose, even as she took the cord from her neck. Opening the jar, she tipped it and waited for the luxurious ointment to pour into her palm. Nothing came forth. Impulsively, hands shaking with impatience at the reluctance of the nard to flow, she struck the neck of the fragile vial against a nearby stone basin. As the alabaster shattered into glistening shards, the nard was freed from its luminous prison and she poured it urgently over Jesus' head, anointing him with the healing balm. Meeting with his body's warmth, the ointment ran gently over his face and hair. Its fragrance filled the room and appeared to soothe him.

Just as quickly as the fragrance engulfed the space, an argument erupted about the extravagance of this gesture, a ritual reserved for bridegrooms, prophets, royalty—and for the Expected One. To those assembled this was an outrage and they scolded her severely as if she were a child. No one noticed as Jesus turned to face the woman.

Why do you trouble her? She has done what she could in ministering to me. She has anticipated what must be done when I am gone.

As he spoke, she was awestruck by the deeper meaning of his words. *He warns them not to question the generosity of my spirit or my ability to give out of what is mine to give. He defends my need to serve. He affirms the truth of the calling that my heart responds to, as well as my perception of his deepest needs and my own desires. He tells them not to doubt the Wisdom of what I already know must be done for the future.* She looked at him and felt an energy and light penetrate and fill her, as if she were an alabaster jar herself. There was a sense of suspension and slowness in her movement, similar to that of the precious ointment. Her deepest self vibrated with response in such a way as to make her feel as if she might shatter. Flushed and glowing with realization, she cast her eyes down in reverence, hiding a faint smile of gratitude and peace. Doing so, she heard his voice once more.

Truly I tell you, wherever the good news is proclaimed in the whole world, what she has done will be told in remembrance of her.

FOR REFLECTION

In what ways does life's ephemeral nature make itself known to me? What degree of urgency do I feel to respond to the present moment and how do I express it?

Of that which is most precious to me, what also holds me captive? Do I harbor joyful anticipation or reluctant fear as I imagine the possibility of releasing it?

What needs exist in both the human community and the natural world that lure my heart and draw me to action? What is preventing me from pouring out my life to them for the benefit of Creation?

If I am willing to break myself open with extravagant selflessness and generosity of spirit, how is this desire to be manifested in my life? How am I called to serve?

What do I hope will be remembered about me? What will be my legacy?

Because of a Dream

THE WIFE OF PILATE

Now at the festival the governor was accustomed to release a prisoner for the crowd, anyone whom they wanted.

So after they had gathered, Pilate said to them, "Whom do you want me to release for you, Jesus Barabbus or Jesus who is called the Messiah?"

For he realized that it was out of jealousy that they had handed him over.

While he was sitting on the judgment seat, his wife sent word to him, "Have nothing to do with that innocent man, for today I have suffered a great deal because of a dream about him."

Matthew 27:15, 17-19

For days, the air of Jerusalem was charged with a palpable tension. Whether it was the excitement and festivity of the Jews' Passover celebration or the political morass that roiled under the surface of the city's life was difficult to differentiate; both contributed to the wariness of pilgrims and citizens alike. Even in the relative peace and serenity of her household, there was a sense of events unfolding in the region. Palace walls did not shield her from the knowledge of civil and religious unrest beyond their insulating fortification. Occasionally, in private moments, her husband spoke of the tenuous circumstances in which he ruled. She witnessed the inner turmoil caused by his dual roles as husband and governor—one requiring a gentle hand, the other a death grip. She observed a man twisted and contorted by agents beyond his control—and hers.

Her days were spent in the relative luxury of attendance by a variety of servants anticipating her needs. Diversions abounded in the forms of music and food, guests to be entertained, and walks in the enclosed gardens. She bathed in scented waters and applied perfume several times daily. Her bath held shelves lined with pots of unguents, essences in glass bottles, and jars of fragrant oils. Refreshed from her ablutions, her custom was to retreat to the terrace that crowned the palace, where the breezes would complement her feeling of restoration. Depending on where she chose to stand, the elevation provided vistas of the Hinnom and Kidron valleys located beyond the walls of Jerusalem. Here, her mind was released to fly over the Temple Mount and come to rest in the lush olive groves opposite. This was her place of solitude and freedom, where she felt unencumbered by the requirements of her station in life. Here her imagination could roam as it had when she was a young girl.

If she dropped her line of sight, however, there were more mundane and disturbing views. The masses of people below revealed their humble status in life. She could see the beggars waiting upon paltry alms they hoped would be offered. There were the occasional street scuffles between would-be thieves and the palace guard. She saw women bearing children on their hips and the weight of difficult lives on their shoulders. And, much closer, she was able to see the proceedings of the praetorium below the terrace. The huge, striated stone blocks that constituted the floor of this court seemed small from this distance, yet they formed the backdrop of a place feared for the immensity of the proceedings that took place within its confines. It was a place of judgment and sentence, where her husband's word could exact the most terrible of punishments—even death.

Collectively, these were often the sights that invaded her sleep and drew her attention inward to contemplate the seemingly irreconcilable extremes of the world around her: wealth and poverty; comfort and hardship; innocence and guilt; truth and deceit.

This was such a night. Images of the familiar and the bizarre filled her dream world. What she recognized became frightful out of context; the unusual piqued her dream-self with curiosity and led her further into this ephemeral world. Surfacing abruptly into consciousness, she gasped for air and looked around. The liminal space between the dream world and reality was blurred; there was no clue to tell which world she inhabited. *My heart pounds within my breast; I live. Breathe. Be calm. Yes, this is my chamber. I am safe.* Despite reassuring herself of familiar and tangible surroundings, she felt restive and confused by the portents that remained of her dream. She felt a strong presence of innocence and truth, but had nothing close at hand to which she could tie it. *Why? Is this an omen of threat or a Divine, reassuring message? What is the meaning of this? I am not the one who judges by determining truth and assigning blame! That is the province of my husband, who takes his own counsel in such matters.* So it went for the hours leading to dawn. She held court with her heart and mind, examining images and the strongly felt senses that took their residence within her. *I find no rest! There are no answers, only struggle that leads to more anguish. How do I rid myself of this suffering? Why will the images and sensations not cease to boil within me? What action must I take?*

Light seeped into the shadows of her apartment, heralding a bright and clear morning. Seeking the immediate refreshment of cool air, she stepped out onto the terrace. Standing silently, present to all her heart held, she gradually became aware that the city below was coming to life. Drawn by the sounds of shouting and the swollen murmur of a large crowd, she moved to the balustrade, from where she gazed down into the praetorium. Ahead of a mob that included the chief priests and elders of the Jewish people, pushed like a piece of wood carried to shore by a strong wave, was a man ordinary and humble in appearance. The sight of him struck her with the force of lightning and the magnitude of its energy. She strained to hear the question posed to this man by her husband, asking if he was the King of the Jews. Before the accused could answer, her heart responded: *This is the One my vision foretold. This is the One of truth and innocence!* In that moment, her struggle ceased and the certitude of the necessity for justice engulfed her. She boldly sent word to her husband: *Have nothing to do with that innocent man, for today I have suffered a great deal because of a dream about him.*

Visions and prophecy had always seemed to her to be the realm of the chosen few who were sensitive to the messages and daring enough to risk any consequences that might come from acting on this Wisdom. Now, having interceded for the innocent One, she was conscious of this as her own true identity.

FOR REFLECTION

How can I pay closer attention to the inner workings of my being? By what means am I alerted to God speaking within me?

When I deeply and honestly confront who I am, what is disclosed and brought to conscious awareness? In what ways does the material world help or hinder the revelation of my true identity?

If I encounter confusion and struggle in my life, what benefits might accrue if I willingly remained in the ambiguity of the questions while listening for answers? How can I attune the ears of my heart in preparation for these moments?

How am I called to be a visionary prophet? What awareness or truth do I know in my own depths that, if spoken aloud, would contribute to the unfolding knowledge about the indwelling of the Divine present in the Universe?

Do I trust my inner knowing? Why am I reluctant to share it?

Tears

THE DAUGHTERS OF JERUSALEM

A great number of the people followed him, and among them were women who were beating their breasts and wailing for him.

But Jesus turned to them and said, "Daughters of Jerusalem, do not weep for me, but weep for yourselves and for your children. For the days are surely coming when they will say, 'Blessed are the barren, and the wombs that never bore, and the breasts that never nursed.' Then they will begin to say to the mountains, 'Fall on us'; and to the hills, 'Cover us.'"

Luke 23:27-30

The crowds came for many reasons. Some pursued the horrific spectacle to be entertained, others for reassurance that their own troubles were not so bad. Still more were curious to see this self-proclaimed king for themselves, while there were even those who hoped to observe a miracle. And, among them walked a small band of those who loved this condemned man, their Teacher. No matter what had provoked the crowds, however, they were now drawn to follow the drama to its completion by a common, unseen, yet tangible, energy.

The ragged procession through the streets of Jerusalem could be seen and heard from a great distance. Brown, languid dust hung over its course in clouds that mirrored the darkness of the approaching storm. The stillness of the air was pierced with feminine ululations that echoed between building walls and re-verberated in the center of each listener's heart. Sobs and shouts punctuated the atmosphere, but it was the constant trill of the women's wailing that announced the nearness of execution and the collective helplessness to act against it. At the beginning, outside the praetorium, its pitch and tenor rose and fell. But as the elevation of the ground under them gradually rose with their approach to the place called The Skull, so did the intensity of the sound.

Every individual, from youth to old age, knew this sound. It ushered in the new life of a wedding with celebratory rhythm; however, in the face of death, the sound transformed itself into a mournful cadence. Layering voice upon voice, alternating wail after wail as they walked immediately behind the Cyrenean who carried the crosspiece for the condemned man, the women ac-companied Jesus of Nazareth to his fate.

Together, they advanced slowly in the wake of the Teacher's weak and staggered steps, only to stop completely as he turned to face them. So unexpected was this action that their ululations abruptly ceased, the women staring in amazement as Jesus found breath to speak.

Daughters of Jerusalem, do not weep for me, but weep for yourselves and for your children. For the days are surely coming when they will say, "Blessed are the barren, and the wombs that never bore, and the breasts that never nursed." Then they will begin to say to the mountains, "Fall on us"; and to the hills, "Cover us."

As Jesus moved away from them, the women did not follow. Shocked into stillness, their wailing and weeping silenced, they looked to one another with questioning eyes, their feet rooted to the ground they stood upon. They stood as pebbles in a stream, the waters of the crowd surging around them until at last they remained alone.

Finding their feet once more, the women began to trail after the crowd. Thoughts, insights, remembered passages from the Scriptures, and questions tumbled through their minds and crashed against one another, as they walked and spoke to one another in low whispers.

He called us "Daughters of Jerusalem." In the great Song of Solomon, the Daughters of Jerusalem asked questions and held secrets. Why, then, should we weep for ourselves and our children? What does his caution mean? He tells us not to announce death for him; does that mean we will soon die? Remember the words of the prophet Hosea: "Ephraim's glory shall fly away like a bird—no birth, no pregnancy, no conception!" Perhaps, but therein may be the secret his words hold. A woman's worth lies in her ability to bring children forth into the world, yet he says that the time will come when barrenness will be extolled. Is it possible that with this knowledge, we can defy what may come? The Scriptures say, "I have set before you life and death, blessings and curses. Choose life so that you and your descendents may live." He urged us not to cry over him and what has already been done, but to cry with tears of joy, as at a wedding, for ourselves and our children, for all children. He urges to use our voices for life and not death! Those who inflict destruction upon the people and the land hide under the mountains and hills because of their guilt. They refuse the responsibility of love, which mothers accept and know so well. He asks us to come out of hiding and not allow ourselves to be emptied of life. How will we respond to this call of his? We must teach the generations to come of the power to be found in life! Surely, Holy Wisdom resides within our breasts, our wombs and our hearts and longs to be poured out into the world!

Having contemplated and voiced all of this, the women now stood once again in silence, this time facing the precipice of death. With defiant courage, they supported each other in the mutual embrace of an awareness that reverenced the Wisdom of their sharing, as well as that which had been revealed to them of their power to choose life for the future of the world.

FOR REFLECTION

With whom do I share my experiences of Divine Wisdom and the questions that arise within me from these encounters? What blessings or challenges do I receive in these conversational exchanges?

What do I believe is the power of shared energy, right now, in effecting changes upon the trajectory of life for future generations? How do I enlarge my capacity for empathy and cooperation in order to be able to share and receive more readily?

What insights concerning the future have I already arrived at as the result of Wisdom-sharing? What questions remain to be contemplated and shared?

What does it mean to receive new life and to nurture it to fullness in my life, in the world, and in the universe? Which parts of the paradigm out of which I live need to expand or contract in order to accommodate the fullness of life?

When I have before me the choice between what is life-giving and what is death-dealing, where do I choose to stand and with whom? What are the implications of my choice?

Witness

THE GALILEAN WOMEN

There were also women looking on from a distance; among them were Mary Magdalene, and Mary the mother of James the younger and of Joses, and Salome.

These used to follow him and provided for him when he was in Galilee; and there were many other women who had come up with him to Jerusalem.

Mark 15:40-41

Meanwhile, standing near the cross of Jesus were his mother, and his mother's sister, Mary the wife of Clopas, and Mary Magdalene.

When Jesus saw his mother and the disciple whom he loved standing beside her, he said to his mother, "Woman, here is your son." Then he said to the disciple, "Here is your mother." And from that hour the disciple took her into his own home.

John 19:25-27

Awide phalanx of ordinary people, soldiers, rocks, and fetid air stood between them and the cross upon which their beloved Jesus now hung. Because their own numbers, though considerable, were relatively small compared with the assembled crowd, they clung to one another—a knot of feminine presence and energy that refused to be displaced. His mother and the beloved disciple stood at their center like a heart pulsing with a sustaining rhythm for all the women, as well as for the crucified One whom they loved. They endured the sight of blood and the gasps of pain with the wisdom and patience of midwives who could see beyond the immediate moment to a radically different future. They saw beyond the nakedness of the man to the naked innocence of the child, who had been welcomed into the embrace of his mother many years ago. As they looked into one another's eyes, an unspoken sense that they were witnessing the birth of something much more powerful than anything they could possibly imagine passed back and forth among them. It was evident to each woman that the overwhelming, final stage of labor to give birth to something new was at work under the outward appearance of the throes of death. Each woman's body and spirit recognized the process of birth.

Their journey to this place of birth had taken them far from their homes and work in the Galilee. They had made a choice to follow this man Jesus—this son of the woman around whom they now stood as bulwark and source of strength. They had shared the means and resources that were theirs to give willingly over the course of the past few years. They had instructed their households to serve as welcoming refuges for him, in order to shield him from the pressing crowds and the demands of his ministry. Their domestic tables had welcomed Jesus and his disciples with nourishment and friendship, just as their means procured provisions for sustenance while they traveled across the various districts. They withheld nothing at their disposal.

Even now, as the storm gathered over Golgotha and whipped their garments around them, the women gave themselves as witnesses to the birth occurring before them, ensuring the generations yet to be born would recall and recount the details of it. Despite the chaos that reigned in the throng of onlookers, a silent mandate was given to these followers of Jesus to remember every minute of these hours of labor and delivery. It would be the account of this time as witnessed by the women who stood on that forsaken hill that would stand as testimony to the depth of Divine Love for Creation. Thus, they remained—attentive, vulnerable, self-possessed.

As time wore on, Jesus began to utter the words of the psalm: *My God, my God, why have you forsaken me?* Despite the energy shared with him by the women present, his body could not summon the strength to continue the prayer. Instead, the feminine voices of heart and tongue carried it forward. The women knew it well because of their own travails: *Why are you so far from helping me, from the words of my groaning? O my God, I cry by day, but you do not answer; and by night, but find no rest. "Let God deliver—let God rescue the one in whom God delights!" Yet, it was you who took me from the womb; you kept me safe on my mother's breast. On you I was cast from my birth, and since my mother bore me you have been my God. Future generations will be told about the Lord, and proclaim his deliverance to a people yet unborn.*

With the time of deliverance imminent, Jesus looked to the woman who had kept him safe as a child on her breast. Once again, she held him with a gaze of infinite strength and love. He responded in submissive obedience, acknowledging himself to be the fulfillment of her openness to Holy Wisdom, to the Spirit of God: *Woman, here is your son.* Defiled, abused, crucified—he was and always would be her son. Then, with an even greater effort to form the words, Jesus turned to the disciple whom he loved, the one with whom he had shared the energy of life, and entrusted his mother into her care: *Here is your mother.*

Receiving one another as gift, they embraced each other as Jesus surrendered his spirit to the Domain of the Divine. They would eventually return to his home to mourn and heal. Even though the future birthed at the moment of his death was incomprehensible to them, the love they had known with him during his life still filled their hearts with a cadence of renewed strength and courage. Along with the many women who stood with them, they witnessed blood and water pour forth from his side—the fluids that ushered in a new life. Midwives all, they stood ready to receive the body of Jesus and to tell all who would desire to know how this new life came into the world.

FOR REFLECTION

When were the times in my life when prayer and silent witness were the only words I could utter? If I were called upon now to articulate what those moments were like, how might I describe them?

How has my image of the Divine changed over the years? Through what circumstances of life have I experienced myself as a midwife who was called upon to assist in birthing a new understanding of God's presence in the world?

Is it possible that I have knowingly or unknowingly withheld the means and resources that are mine to give for the benefit of others and the whole of Creation? By what means am I able to cultivate a personal culture of generosity?

What events have I witnessed that enlarged my consciousness of the Divine at work in the Universe? How will I communicate my experience to those future generations who have not yet heard the story of God's great love for the world?

What strengths of character do I possess that allow me to create a welcoming home within my heart for the unwanted and unexpected? Who has been entrusted to my care in the hope and with the anticipation of a compassionate embrace? How have I responded?

Sitting in the Dirt

MARY OF MAGDALA

When it was evening, there came a rich man from Arimathea, named Joseph, who was also a disciple of Jesus.

He went to Pilate and asked for the body of Jesus; then Pilate ordered it to be given to him.

So Joseph took the body and wrapped it in a clean linen cloth and laid it in his own new tomb, which he had hewn in the rock. He then rolled a great stone to the door of the tomb and went away.

Mary Magdalene and the other Mary were there, sitting opposite the tomb.

Matthew 27:57-61

The man she loved was dead. The man she had welcomed into her life, into her home, into her heart, was gone. Just as she had walked next to him in life, so had she stood vigil throughout his slow and anguished dying. At the end, she embraced him with her spirit, holding him in the only way she could as he surrendered his own spirit into the hands of his Abba. Now, her strength spent, she sat down in the dust in defiance of law and faith, staring at a stone which barred her from the one she loved.

Was it only a few hours ago that she last looked into his eyes to give him strength—the strength that comes only when you peer deeply into the eyes of the one you love? It seemed an instant and an eternity had passed since that moment. Thoughts and memories invaded her exhausted mind and overwhelmed heart. Their meals together in Bethany; his laughter during celebrations; the sound of his voice as he taught; the gentle, reassuring touch of his hand on her skin; the sense of his nearness; his look across the heads of the crowd; his defense of her as she had anointed him. His words echoed within her: *The Son of Man will be raised on the third day.* The hope of his promise rooted her to the ground where she sat and riveted her eyes to the stone she willed to move and release the one she loved—just as on a day long ago he had commanded a stone be moved for a brother's release from Sheol.

Hers was a faithful presence now, a faithfulness she would not allow death to destroy. She would remain in this place when others had left out of fear; this man's mother her only companion. With each beat of her heart, the sun slipped closer to the horizon, closer to Sabbath. She would dare to stay as long as possible. *How can I leave him? Surely, a piece of me will be left behind when I go. Truly, a part of myself has also died and been entombed with the Beloved.* Her mind reeled. *Yet, on the third day…* the words stirred her heart and roused her courage. *Is Love strong enough to break the bindings of death?* Her heart cried out from its depths. *What do I feel? Is it the presence of his love? Is this what moves and rises within me? Yes, if something of me has died, then, in spite of tombs and stones, something of him remains alive!*

In the crimson wash of dying sunlight, she relinquished her watchfulness to exhaustion and the Sabbath. She struggled to her feet and, with a gesture born of intimacy, gently touched the stone in front of her. Then, with the same hand, she reached out for the older woman next to her—supporting her as together they walked into the deepening stillness of the approaching Sabbath's first hour. Already, she felt the presence of Love that would call her faithful heart back to the tomb before the Light of the third day returned.

FOR REFLECTION

*What bars me from fully embracing what I love?
How am I called to be present to what I love despite
obstacles?*

*From what have I sought release in my life? What do I
seek to release from my life?*

*When I am rooted and grounded in hope, how do I
manifest this perspective in my life? To whom or what
am I abidingly faithful? How does hope strengthen my
commitment?*

*Who has companioned me in facing the seemingly
insurmountable obstacles of my life? Who have I
companioned under similar circumstances? How have
these relationships added dimension and depth to my
life?*

*What moves and rises within me? What does this
movement compel me to acknowledge in my life?*

Preeminent Choice

JOANNA

Soon afterwards he went on through cities and villages, proclaiming and bringing the good news of the kingdom of God.

The twelve were with him, as well as some women who had been cured of evil spirits and infirmities: Mary, called Magdalene…and Joanna, the wife of Herod's steward Chuza, and Susanna, and many others, who provided for them out of their resources.

Luke 8:1-3

It was now about noon, and darkness came over the whole land until three in the afternoon, while the sun's light failed; and the curtain of the temple was torn in two.

He breathed his last.

The women who had followed him from Galilee, stood at a distance, watching these things.

Then they remembered his words, and returning from the tomb, they told all this to the eleven and to all the rest. Now it was Mary Magdalene, Joanna, Mary the mother of James, and the other women with them who told this to the apostles.

Luke 23:44-46, 49; 24:8-10

Two days ago, the ground rumbled and shook beneath her feet in much the same way it had three years before, when her journey to the mount called Golgotha began. As she stood on the storm-lashed hillside, she noted how remarkably similar the present tremors passing beneath her feet were to those she had previously felt—when the quaking earth had precipitated an upheaval in the very ground of her being. In imitation of the earth, she had made a choice then that fractured what had been a solid structure of husband, home, and accustomed place in society. It set her irrevocably on a path that wound circuitously from the known to the unknown, until it led her to that forsaken outcropping of rock. There she stood, through the protracted hours of the Teacher's agonized passage into the arms of death, with the other women who had accompanied him from Galilee. Shaken violently by the scene of brutal desolation before her eyes, she wondered what else would break open in her life.

It seemed long ago when she had watched each sunrise in Tiberias rival its predecessor, when waves of muted color seeped over the horizon and echoed the gentle lapping waters at the shoreline of the Kinneret. The lake and all the residents who gazed upon its many moods from the elite precincts of the Herodian court were known variously by Roman, Aramaic, and Hebrew names, vestiges of life new and old. The city of Herod Antipas itself rose up from the ruins of an almost-forgotten village to become the shining epicenter of a new tetrarchy and its government; yet, its foundations desecrated an ancient cemetery and defiled those who dared to enter. In this place of stark contrasts, she lived a privileged existence as the wife of the king's steward. Its luxuries, however, did not hide the obvious, hateful sentiments of the Galilean people—her people—toward the Herodian court's insistence on the trappings of Roman life and the burdensome imposition of the taxation that sustained it. The truth of her situation was that, for most of her years, she existed between the two worlds of religious heritage and social class—and did not truly belong to either. In the end, it may have been precisely this sense of ambivalence that allowed her to make what would become the preeminent choice of her life. A desire for purpose and belonging—beyond the role and relationship of wife to husband—permeated her tenuous existence in Tiberias.

Situated on the Via Maris, the Way of the Sea, Tiberias was a locus of the trade route that stretched from Mesopotamia to Egypt. Caravans of vendors and ordinary travelers frequented the city, creating an exciting and dangerous mix of people and cultures. News from the world was exchanged in the markets and on the streets, in the baths and the amphitheater, as well as in the court of Herod. Rumors travelled in similar fashion, only with greater speed; and so she had heard of the approach of a man who roamed the Galilee attended by his disciples, along with large crowds of the poor and the merely curious. It was said he possessed the power to heal and his teaching spoke of a Domain of peace and love, distinct from the Pax Romana—the peace of Rome, which was founded upon power and assimilation.

Upon hearing confirmation of the Teacher's arrival, she did not deliberate long before leaving the confines of the court. Surreptitiously, she followed the urgings of her heart to the outskirts of the city and there dissolved into the masses listening to the Teacher's words. Looking back to that day, she understood now there was no one word or gesture of healing that had compelled her heart. Rather, it was everything—the tone of his voice, the Wisdom he imparted through his words, the gentle compassion for those who had lost hope, the attentiveness of the women and men who were his disciples.

Gradually, she realized she saw a reflection of herself in some of the Teacher's women disciples. They possessed means and resources similar to hers, evident in the way they carried themselves and the quality of their dress. Their faces revealed the light of intelligence. *But there is something else…something more in the way they conduct themselves. Confidence? Yes, but not that alone. What is it that I perceive in their eyes? They are attentive and aware of every sound uttered by the Teacher. Their bodies show no sign of tension, of course, for they are accustomed to independence. Ah, could that be? Do they actually feel the peace of which the Teacher speaks? Do they know freedom in his presence? How is it possible that in belonging to this gathering of disparate people one would find the peace of true freedom?*

Her searching heart pondered the value of such freedom and knew it almost instantly to be worth all that was rightfully hers to give, including every denarii of her ketubah and dowry, as well as deeds of gift received earlier in her life. *Little did I know those many years ago that the means and property set aside for support in my wisdom years would now provide sustenance for so many more. Yet, I give it gladly and without reservation. It is the least of my resources, substantial as it may be. I also choose to give something far greater than wealth. I dedicate the whole of my energy and being to the way of the Teacher, to attentiveness to his word, and to sharing the insights of Wisdom. I will accompany him wherever he leads me.*

Vibrations emanating from deep inside the earth had met her words of commitment that day. The world as she had known it heaved around her and catapulted her onto the path of Jesus' itinerant life. It was a route strewn with hardship, misunderstanding, and unaccustomed service. Despite its obstacles, she travelled it with dignity and fortitude. Tender care and defense of the weak were resources she offered frequently, along with acceptance and tolerance. She learned to speak in a manner that invited others to weigh the truth of her words and discover the way of the Teacher for themselves.

The flood of recollections primed her mind and heart, each

wave of memory pushing her closer and closer to the present moment until, at last, she stood before the empty tomb. Perplexed, she and the other women attuned themselves to hear any sound that might ground them in the reality of what had happened—what was still happening. What they heard resonated with authority and moved them to reverence the energy present to them: *Remember, how he told you.*

Remember. Consumed by the certain knowledge of the fulfillment of the Teacher's words, she summoned forth an intrinsic capacity to witness convincingly to the new reality. She spoke and allowed her testimony to be assessed and tested by the men to whom she and the other women had carried it. Whether these men would receive it as idle chatter or as the very truth spoken by the Teacher remained to be seen.

The truth of my choice is that I followed my heart. I listened to the One who moved me with words of Truth, who was Truth in his very essence. I chose compassion when it was presented against the backdrop of opulence and prestige. I do not regret this choice that changed my life, for I know that I am suffused with the Divine energy of Love. I belong to a reality far greater than myself. I am free.

FOR REFLECTION

In my life, when have I felt that the world crumbled around me and the ground under me was shaken by events beyond my immediate control? How did I respond? How will I respond if I am presented with such a challenge again?

When choices present themselves, who or what do I rely upon in making a decision? Do I trust and consult my own wisdom and inner urgings? How do I integrate the various perspectives?

At what point(s) in my life have I felt that I existed between two worlds—and did not truly belong to either? How did I seek resolution to the dilemma(s) and what, in turn, have I learned?

What am I searching for that I feel is lacking in or missing from my life now? Am I willing to walk beyond my comfort zone to discover what I need?

What are my definitions of personal and spiritual freedom? What would truly free me to be my authentic self?

Known and Called by Name

MARY OF MAGDALA

Early on the first day of the week, while it was still dark, Mary Magdalene came to the tomb and saw that the stone had been removed from the tomb.

Mary stood weeping outside the tomb. As she wept, she bent over to look into the tomb and she saw two angels.

They said to her, "Woman why are you weeping?"

She said to them, "They have taken away my Lord, and I do not know where they have laid him."

When she had said this, she turned around and saw Jesus standing there, but she did not know that it was Jesus.

Jesus said to her, "Woman, why are you weeping? Whom are you looking for?"

Then Jesus said to her, "Mary!"

She turned and said to him, "Rabbouni!"

Jesus said to her, "Do not hold on to me. Go to my brothers."

Mary Magdalene went and announced to the disciples, "I have seen the Lord!"

John 20:1, 11-18

Overhead, the lights of heaven nodded to her with a soft pulsation. In this hour before dawn, when the world held its breath awaiting the new day, these small points of light reassured her with their presence. The storms of the previous day had passed; the sky now possessed the appearance of onyx, rich and black, which only made the profusion of stars strewn across it more stunning. The blackness, however, could also conceal unknown terrors in its shadows and empty spaces, which provoked a guarded wariness in her. As the darkness enveloped her, a woman alone, it tried to extinguish the light she carried in her heart—a small, yet steady, flame of love. This small glow was enough for the eyes of her heart to see by; its illumination guided her feet over the rough ground and gave her courage to confront the spirits of Sheol that might roam in the night.

She arrived in the garden where they had laid him in the tomb, pausing just long enough to be certain of the exact place. Anticipation and trepidation vied within her and her mind traveled momentarily to the story of the matriarch Rebekah, whose twins wrestled in her belly for the right to be first-born. Seeing the stone rolled away from the tomb entrance, her instincts told her to escape and find those who would believe the testimony of what was now her greatest fear.

Jesus' disciples had taken refuge in a nearby home, where she arrived out of breath and heart pounding wildly: *He has been taken from the tomb, and I do not know where his body is!*

Upon hearing her words, two of the disciples started for the tomb, at first running side by side, but she saw from behind that the younger reached it first. After what seemed to her an endless, hesitant pause, this pair of disciples entered the tomb one at a time, their love for Jesus having conquered their own fears. However, each having found only the winding cloths of burial, still perfumed by the mixture of myrrh and aloe, the two turned in resignation to leave the tomb and go back to their beds. Flames of anger surged to the surface from primal recesses deep within her and she screamed after them: *No! Fools, you cannot leave! You cannot return to your beds! Don't you understand the words of the prophets? Don't you understand who he is?*

As she watched the receding shapes of the two dissolve into the darkness, tears welled in her eyes and spilled down her face, anointing the ground outside the tomb. With the fire of her anger quelled by these tiny drops of life-giving water, she surrendered to the flood of despair she had held at bay. It was impossible to believe he was truly gone, when so recently he had been close enough to touch. Closing her eyes, she thought she could still feel his energy and warmth.

Yet, in an interior place still deeper than she could have imagined, the power of love fanned the embers of courage and hope once more—stirring them into a bright light. She stared at the gaping mouth of the tomb and cursed its emptiness…and her own. *Every fiber of my being is repulsed by this blackness. How different from the sky that cradles the lights of hope.* Yet, one step at a time, she felt herself drawn down into the tomb. Mystery suffused the space. Two beings, as if formed of light, emanated compassion and peace. Aware of this presence, she heard one speak: *Woman, why are you weeping?* A wail of mourning erupted inside of her. *Why am I weeping? Why? I am lost without him and do not know how to recover his presence!*

Desolate, she turned away from the tomb. In doing so, she was startled by the figure of a man standing no more than an arm's length away. She assumed him to be a caretaker of the garden. Diverting her eyes in a gesture of respect, she heard him ask the same question: *Woman, why are you weeping? Whom are you looking for?*

Please, if you are the one who took him away, or if you saw those who did, I beg you to tell me where the body is, and I will take him away. A moment of silence passed between them.

Mary? Hearing her name called so gently, she raised her head. Looking deeply into her tearful eyes, Jesus once again called her by name—*Mary!* Waves of morning light broke the horizon, sending a palpable vibration into the garden around her. Colors burst forth and the caress of light stirred the trees to liveliness in the warm air. Songbirds burst forth with melodies. The liturgy of the renewed day emerged and with it her heart resonated with energy. It was as if her name had been uttered by the Source of Love with a power that freed her from an unknown, secret bondage.

Although she experienced a strong urge to touch him for the simple reassurance that he was truly present, the joy of it all and the need to exult in sharing this good news overwhelmed her. Remarkable in the midst of this was her recollection of a liturgical tradition that required lamentations preceding a Divine message delivered by a prophet. She had shed her tears, and now no longer in tears, she turned to the rising sun and walked into the liturgy of the day as prophet and apostle of the Christ.

FOR REFLECTION

Can I identify the dark nights that have occurred in my life? Who or what were the pinpoints of light for me in that darkness?

To give birth to a new reality, implies letting go of a known one. What frightens me about becoming the fully empowered person I am intended to be?

How have I had to confront fear over the course of my lifetime? If I allow myself to go down into the depths of my fears, what do I expect to find or learn there?

In what ways do my fears prevent me at times from moving in a new, energizing direction? By opening myself to the possibility that a deeper knowing will result from a change in perspective, why would I ever countenance allowing fear to hold me back?

God knows my true name. When I hear myself called by this name, do I recognize it and give myself permission to respond? How does my true name empower me?

Heart on Fire

THE WOMAN ON THE ROAD TO EMMAUS

Meanwhile, standing near the cross of Jesus were his mother, and his mother's sister, Mary the wife of Clopas, and Mary Magdalene.

John 19:25

Now on that same day two of them were going to a village called Emmaus, about seven miles from Jerusalem, and talking with each other about all these things that had happened. While they were talking and discussing, Jesus himself came near and went with them, but their eyes were kept from recognizing him. And he said to them, "What are you discussing with each other as you walk along?" They stood still, looking sad. Then one of them, whose name was Cleopas, answered him…

As they came near the village to which they were going, Jesus walked ahead as if he were going on. But they urged him strongly, saying, "Stay with us, because it is almost evening and the day is now nearly over." So he went in to stay with them. When he was at table with them, he took bread, blessed and broke it, and gave it to them. Then their eyes were opened, and they recognized him. They said to each other, "Were not our hearts burning within us while he was talking to us on the road, while he was opening the scriptures to us?"

Luke 24:13-18, 28-32

The weather of the first month was unpredictable as always. Only yesterday, as she stood on Golgotha, the sudden storm lashed out in fury at the obscenity of the crucifixion. The number of women with her was few, yet they proved formidable opponents to the wind and lightning that sought to drive them away. Huddled in shawls, she and the other women defied the desire of the weather to mourn in solitude; the deep energy of their hearts rooted them to the rocky ground in the same way an ancient tree takes hold and stands firm. Unmoving, she watched as the Teacher surrendered his life into the all-encompassing energy of his Abba's love. Her mind's eye was etched with the image of Jesus' broken body in the same way the lightning left a phantom image behind her physical eyes—stark in contrast to her memories of his living energy.

She knew only emotional upheaval and exhaustion after witnessing the execution—a mixture that did not allow her to settle into the rest and peace of Sabbath. She lay awake the same night wondering how she would recover sufficiently in order to attempt the journey home with her husband, Clopas, after the conclusion of Sabbath. She imagined the prayer of Havdalah, which would mark the end of this sacred time of Shabbat, its candle flame reflected on the surface of the cup of wine and the fragrance of spices suffusing the air. Meant to allow the memories of Shabbat to be carried into the ordinary time of the week, the sweet warmth of the wine would trickle down her throat. Now, however, for the first time in her life the thought of this prayer was too much to conceive. This Sabbath's memories were fraught with images that convulsed her spirit. Desolation and emptiness lapped at the edges of her mind. She knew the burdens of loss and longing would be heavy, yet there seemed to be no memories that would quicken the steps of her journey home—a journey that would take a full day to complete.

Despite her apprehension, the first day of the week dawned

quiet and bright as she and Clopas started for their village of Emmaus. Even while others choked the road leading from Jerusalem to return to their own homes after the Passover festival, there were brief intervals that allowed for intimate conversation between wife and husband. The monotony of their steps produced a fluid sense of time and place; their shared recollections of recent events returned them to the vivid reality of it all once more—sweat, blood, wailing, prayerful invocations, cursing, sounds of strangled breath, the outline of the cross against the blackness of the storm. They whispered to one another of fear and heartbreak, as fatigue stole over her with the passing hours. The undulating, muddy slopes of the track commanded what little attention she still possessed. It became difficult to focus beyond the next step and this prevented her from noticing when another traveler approached.

This stranger walked nearby and only acknowledged them with a silent nod of his head. It was some time before he spoke with apparent curiosity. *What are you discussing with each other as you walk along?* Shocked by this man's direct inquiry, wife and husband stopped in unison and looked at one another, each holding the sadness of the other tenderly. Simultaneously, questions rose in her consciousness and her eyes urged her husband to be cautious in responding. *Who is he? Why has he chosen to speak to us of all the people on this road? How can he not know of the events that stirred the city into frenzy? Do we dare reveal our relationship to our beloved Teacher, Jesus, and what we know of his identity?*

Ignorant of the man's origins, her husband introduced himself in the universal language of trade—as Cleopas, the Greek variation of his name. Questions and answers were exchanged among the three, allowing trepidation to give way slowly to growing boldness. Forgetting public propriety, wife and husband together soon conveyed for this stranger all they knew of what had transpired. Their admiration for the executed Prophet was evident, as was their intense and incredulous disappointment with the lack of vision and Wisdom on the part of the chief priests and elders who abandoned him to torture and death. The traveler's response to their revelations shocked her with its caustic tone, as he accused them of foolishness and slowness of heart. *I know the ways of my heart! It opens itself readily to be filled with Wisdom. It responds instantly to the language of love and compassion. How does this stranger dare to accuse my righteous heart?*

No longer was she aware of each step on this journey home. A new vigor ignited her and engulfed her as this man, who possessed the bearing and tongue of a rabbi, recalled the Scriptures that told of the Expected One, the suffering servant spoken of by the prophet Isaiah. The remaining distance dissolved in a curious mixture of voices and memories. Each passage of the Scriptures that he recited called forth scenes long held in the sanctuary of her heart, yet so real she imagined Jesus before her once again at table, teaching on a hillside—even admiring the grain of a piece of wood in his father's workplace. Her recollections were overwhelming in number and she felt warm in their presence, as if the jostling of them within her threw off small sparks of fire that inflamed her exhausted body. The more she attuned herself to the traveler's voice and words, the greater was the sense of comforting and restorative heat.

As the sun slipped toward the horizon and they arrived at last in Emmaus, she and her husband urged their companion to share with them at table in thanksgiving for the safe journey. Having been away from her hearth for some time, there were few provisions at hand. She prepared a simple meal of the bread she had carried from Jerusalem and wine. They welcomed the presence of their guest by affording him the honor of breaking the bread to share between them. His manner of breaking the crust and handing it to them, pouring the wine and passing the cup, was intriguingly familiar. *Where have I known this gesture before? Who might have…?* She broke off in sudden realization of who sat at table with them. *This is not possible! My eyes may deceive me, but surely the Wisdom of my heart knows beyond doubt that this is Jesus the Christ!* Turning to her husband, she saw the same recognition dawning on his face as he looked toward her. How long they searched one another's faces for confirmation of the truth of this man's identity was impossible to determine, but when at last they broke away from their mutual gaze, the man who was no longer a stranger to them had gone.

Were not our hearts burning within us while he was talking to us on the road, while he was opening the Scriptures to us? Why did I not trust the sensations of warm memory and the Wisdom of my heart's knowing? Memory burst suddenly into flaming energy as her consciousness opened to a greater understanding of what this experience would exact from her. Long before this day, Jesus had sent out pairs of his disciples to speak of the Domain of God—now, she and her husband would return to the women and men remaining in Jerusalem to speak of this good news and to stir the embers of memories smothered by fear.

FOR REFLECTION

What deep energy within me serves as an anchor in my life? How trusting am I of the sensations of warm memory and the Wisdom of my heart's knowing for guidance in life?

When do I allow myself to experience Sabbath moments that restore my energy and clarify my vision? Why do I relinquish fulfilling my need for this refreshment so readily?

What makes it difficult for me to focus beyond the next step of my journey? What prevents me from noticing others as they approach me?

How do my memories enliven and energize me? When images from my past materialize in front of my mind's eye, what glimpse of the Divine appears simultaneously?

Who is Jesus for me? What does my encounter with him empower within me?

AFTERWORD

Each woman in this book discovered and revealed her voice, her power, and her authenticity, as well as her path in life, through an encounter with Jesus—Prophet, Teacher, Healer, Storyteller, Messiah.

Each woman was empowered as a unique expression of Divine energy through an exchange of that same energy with Jesus.

Each woman was a being of potential waiting for the moment of enlightenment to become more fully the person who God desired her to be, set afire with energy and light.

Each woman is an expression of some part of us as individuals. As we become aware of and empowered by our own portion of the Divine energy that suffuses all of Creation, each woman's story in this book will be brought to completion.

ACKNOWLEDGMENTS

From the time of my earliest memories to the present moment, it is apparent to me that I have always felt the call to challenge and make sense of the disconcerting and confusing elements of life. Even as a little girl, I wanted to know the reasons behind what I encountered. I am (still) blessed by my parents, Berni and Don Dehn, who have always counseled critical thinking, creativity, and the pursuit of excellence. I can hear my mother's voice telling me and my three sisters years ago, "You can be anything you want to be in life!" She consistently urged me to write and gifted me with the opportunity to develop my faith and spirituality. In a similar manner, my father introduced me to a wide variety of disciplines such as archeology, anthropology, and astronomy. He helped me understand the great variety in the expression of human beliefs. I am grateful to both of them for always nurturing my curious spirit.

Theodora Pochowicz, my maternal grandmother, was also a formative influence on my life. Hers was a spirit combined of faith, courage, energy, independence, and Wisdom. She was a source of unconditional love for me and taught me so much about the feminine face of the Divine.

My daughters, Krisan and Keri, are my greatest joys in life. I am in awe of the beautiful, talented women they have become—women who follow their hearts with confidence and share their gifts with the world. They listened deeply and honored my desire to articulate feminine perspective, experience, and emotion in the stories of the women who were ignored, forgotten, or silenced in the canonical Scriptures. It was their encouragement that urged me to continue writing even when fatigue or frustration got the better of me. Both read drafts of my work with critical eyes and a mutual love for the written word. Most importantly, they were the inspiration for this book.

I am grateful for the support of a special group of women whose Wisdom-sharing, insights, love, and prayers have been my sustenance for years and who graciously accompanied me throughout the creative journey of this book: Ellin Christensen, Barb Foreman, Jackie Goes, Lisa Goes, and Jane Zimmerman. Together, they encouraged me to see this work to completion. I must also note with special gratitude the gift of spiritual energy I received from Barb Foreman, who always challenged me to greater clarity and depth of vision.

There have been many sources of inclusive, feminine Wisdom for me over the years in the women's religious congregations. I am especially indebted to the women of the Sinsinawa and Adrian Dominican Congregations for instilling in me their passion for Truth and Love—which proved to be the foundational energy that acted as a catalyst for me to write this book. My appreciation must also be expressed for the women of the Congregation of Saint Joseph, who continue to provide space for me to marvel at the grace and wonder of the unfolding Sacred Universe and to envision the Divine Domain spoken of by Jesus.

There is really no way to encompass in this note of thanks all of the individuals who persuaded me to write from my heart by telling me about how their own hearts were touched and challenged through my writing in a variety of contexts. This book would not have become reality without each of you.

Finally I must acknowledge my editor and publisher, Greg Pierce, for his faith and trust in my potential as an author. His guidance and support in this endeavor has been invaluable. I am grateful to Greg and to everyone at ACTA Publications who have acted as "midwives" in bringing this book into the world.

ABOUT THE AUTHOR

Susan Dehn Matthews holds a Master of Arts degree in Religious Education and Pastoral Ministry from Mundelein College of Loyola University, Chicago (1979), as well as a Master of Arts in Educational Administration from Dominican University, River Forest (1997). Her areas of professional interest include the history of women's spirituality, Creation-centered spirituality, and Scriptural interpretation and reflection. Trained and certified in spiritual companioning and spiritual direction, Susan is also a certified Pastoral Associate who facilitates a variety of opportunities for Scripture reflection and adult spiritual formation. She writes frequently for parish publications on various topics concerning Scripture and spirituality. Her work, spanning almost four decades, has been diverse, and her ministries include spiritual direction, pastoral counseling, retreat leadership, and creative liturgical planning. As an educator, she has served both as an instructor and as an administrator on the elementary, secondary, and university levels. In recent years, Susan served as a visiting faculty member for the Hesburgh Sabbatical Program at the Catholic Theological Union in Chicago. Additionally, she has presented a variety of workshops and evenings of reflection for parishes and schools in the Chicago area.

A native of the Chicago suburbs, Susan has two adult daughters. In her free time, she enjoys art history, reading, and traveling.

ABOUT THE COVER ART

The watercolor and ink image of "Wisdom" gracing the cover of this book is the work of artist James Fissel. It is a fascinating, complex, and intensely rich translation of the ephemeral and elusive nature of Wisdom. Pivotal in all of Fissel's artwork is the orb. In his own words, Fissel says: "I use the orb as an iconic artistic tool expressing my relationship with the creative spirit, the mystery of life and all the dimensions in the world that exist but cannot be seen." (www.thegoldenorb.net)

When I first encountered "Wisdom", I was struck by the multi-dimensional iconography employed by Fissel, as well as the seamless, unifying quality which existed between these various layers of symbolism. While it is said that beauty lies in the eye of the beholder, perhaps it is also true that meaning is perceived intuitively and viscerally through the contemplation of the work of art by the viewer. Quite apart from what may have been the artist's intention or vision in the creation of this piece, my interpretation of "Wisdom" is essential for the reader to understand the choice of this particular artwork for the cover of this book.

The circular orb that anchors the center of the composition is an ancient and universal symbol of wholeness, infinity, unity, Mother Earth, the cosmos, the Divine, and the Sacred Feminine. Within both the ancient goddess religions and Gnostic Christian traditions, the circle represented female power and was often depicted as a serpent eating its tail.

The ancient Egyptian ankh hieroglyph ☥ conveys myriad meanings, including the balance of female and male power, life, truth, conception, and rebirth. Each woman portrayed in this book, in essence, begins life anew and comes into her power and fullness through an encounter with Jesus. The ankh also connotes holiness and its shape has been assimilated into both Celtic and Coptic Christian crosses. The crosspiece that bisects the painting horizontally forms the curving image of a double axe, which in several world cultures represents matriarchy.

Less obvious to the eye of the observer, is the astrological sign ♀ of Venus. Known as the "Mirror of Venus," it honors the Roman goddess of love and beauty and represents the female element in Creation. Contemporary iconography recognizes it as the symbol of woman. It is not difficult to see in this symbol the crude rendering of a tree, perhaps an oblique nod to the Tree of Life (Knowledge) renowned in the Book of Genesis, or alternately the Tree of Life associated with the ancient Wisdom traditions.

The central orb and the multiple globes held within it are a composite image reminiscent of the womb, with cells entering and subsequently flowing out into the world as new life. The strong vertical movement of the painting, along with the linear design emerging from the orb, speaks of this pathway of birth. The wash of white flowing from top to bottom in this watercolor describes the energy and flow of Divine Wisdom and Spirit, engulfing and flowing through the whole of life. Uniting the composition are the various tones of blue, which appear as the primal waters of life and birth.

–SDM

BOOKS OF RELATED INTEREST

SONG OF THE DOVE
Kay Murdy

An award-winning novel of the life of Mary, Mother of Jesus, from her youth to her death. 258 pages, paperback, $18.95

WOMEN OF THE PASSION
A Novel
Joan D. Lynch

A popular fictionalized version of the time after Jesus' death through the eyes of the women who walked with him. 216 pages, paperback, $14.95

THREE SAINTS
Women Who Changed History
Joan Williams

Stories of three holy women who made real contributions in public life: Genevieve of Paris, Catherine of Siena, and Teresa of Avila. 128 pages, paperback, $9.95

INVITATION TO THE OLD TESTAMENT
INVITATION TO THE NEW TESTAMENT
Alice Camille

Companion books by award-winning author Alice Camille that offer clear, concise, and informative explanations of both the Old and New Testaments. Two 96-page paperbacks, $9.95 each

THE CATHOLIC COMPANION TO MARY
THE CATHOLIC COMPANION TO THE PSALMS
THE CATHOLIC COMPANION TO JESUS
Mary Kathleen Glavich, SND

Three books by noted author and speaker Sr. Kathleen Glavich full of facts, stories, prayers, quotes, places, and pieties about Mary, the Psalms, and Jesus (which won a 2011 book award from the Catholic Press Association). Three 128/176/412-page paperbacks, $9.95/10.95/15.95

Available from Booksellers or 800-397-2282
www.actapublications.com